To Nicolle
With love
Margaret

Bitesize Health

Be Your Best

"Yesterday I was clever, so I wanted to change the world.

Today I am wise, so I am changing myself."

Rumi

M. C. Pardoe

The contents of this book should be used as general guidelines only. Nothing in this book should be taken as medical advice or diagnosis and advice herein is not intended to replace the services of trained health professionals, or be a substitute for medical advice. You are advised to consult with your healthcare professional with regard to matters referring to your health, and in particular regarding matters that may require diagnosis or medical attention. The author does not accept any responsibility for any harm that may occur from your use or misuse of this book or your failure to seek appropriate medical advice.

Health: Bitesize Ways to Change Your Life, Printed by CreateSpace, An Amazon.com Company, Available from Amazon.com and other online stores.

Copyright C 2014 by Margaret Pardoe All rights reserved.
No part of this publication may be reproduced, stored in a retrieval system, or transmitted, in any form or by any means, electronic, mechanical, photocopying, recording or otherwise, without the prior written permission of the author.

Logo design by Jon Bradley

Cover design by Laura Cope.
www.drasticallydigital.co.uk

Acknowledgements

*I was about to acknowledge individually all those who have helped me, either through practical help, emotional support or as a teacher (formally or informally).
Then came the realisation that this list would be longer than the book itself, as absolutely everyone I have ever known falls into one of the above categories!*

*It took a while for me to get there and "get it"!
i.e. to recognise that some of the most negative experiences had the greatest opportunities for learning and healing within them.*

So to everyone who has come into my life: family, friends, teachers, fellow students, clients, patients, acquaintances and everyone else….

*Thank you!
Thank you!!
Thank you!!!*

Forward

This is the book that I wanted to find and read a very long time ago and I waited and waited for someone to write it, until the growing realisation occurred that perhaps that someone is supposed to be me!

It has taken till now for the last pieces of the jigsaw to fall into place and for me to be able to see the bigger picture.

All my life I've been passionate about all aspects of Health:

Mind, Body, Spirit and Emotion.

So why would you want to read on?

Well, because I've spent a very long time learning and researching, and often experiencing, everything I write about.

Every experience has been used to learn and grow.

"Failed to thrive" as a baby; a sickly child; never invincible as a teenager or young adult; lost pregnancies; had cancer scares; raised two wonderful children; been a full-time carer; lived through divorce and bereavement; cheated on in life and love and business; faced financial ruin and recovered….
And a decade ago was told I was "chronically sick and could expect to deteriorate"….
(I'm not and I haven't!).

As a newly qualified nurse on an oncology ward, I dealt with a vast amount of sadness and death. Then the dramatic contrast of happiness and new life as a midwife.

When allopathic medicine failed me personally, I became a naturopathic herbalist and iridologist. And thereafter explored the world of mind/body healing through: The Journey; Neuro-Linguistic Programming (NLP) and Non Personal Awareness (NPA). For several years I practiced as a Journey Accredited Practitioner.

A serial micropreneur, my first small business was at 11 years old.
Then, almost half a century later, graduated with a BA(Hons) in Business Management and Entrepreneurship as a very mature student!
Kind of upside down!

And at the same time as all of this, having an amazing lifetime!

Sailed the seven seas and still exploring as much of this beautiful planet as possible!
Fun and laughter, fear and danger, fabulous highs and crashing lows.
More interesting and exciting than I could ever have dreamed of.

Everything has been used to learn and grow, leaving me with a wealth of knowledge and experience, and hopefully with compassion, empathy, loving kindness and mindfulness.

If my health had been more robust and my life experience less diverse and intense, I believe I would have less motivation to explore all the aspects of health that I am able to share with you now.

All that I've learned, experienced and researched, I'll share with you here. In "bitesize" quantities!

How to Use this Book

Ideally read the complete book first to get an overview and work out your own personal priorities.

Each chapter starts with the potential **Benefits** and an **Action** plan.
If you prefer not to read in-depth initially, you can start by reading the Benefits and Action Plan of your chosen practice.
Then introduce a new topic every few days.

Establish each new practice before starting the next.

At the end of each chapter is a list of resources directing you to further reading, listening or viewing. This enables a topic to be explored in greater depth, with readily accessible information and products signposted.

The lists of Benefits, Action and Resources are a useful aide-memoire as a quick reminder after reading the book.

Prioritise the basics: breathing, eating, drinking, sleeping and moving.
To the best of your personal ability, build a bedrock of physical health.
This will start to improve all aspects of life; e.g. if you smoke it would be wise to stop that first.

Then clean up drinking and eating, followed by fresh air and exercise and getting enough sleep.

The intention is that you integrate each practice into your life as a habit, with each building synergistically on the rest.

CONTENTS

BREATHE 15 - 35

BUGS 37 - 47

DIET 49 – 59

DETOX 61 - 76

DRINK 77 - 97

EARTH 99 - 106

EAT 107 - 127

FAST 129 - 141

FORGIVE 143 - 157

HEAL 159 - 176

LIGHT 177 - 189

MEDITATE 191 – 211

MOVE 213 - 242

SLEEP 243 - 257

THANK 259 - 266

THINK 267 - 278

THE END 279 - 287

BREATHE

BREATHE

BENEFITS

Improving your respiratory function will improve both your general health and fitness, allowing you to physically do so much more!

This is especially significant if you are a smoker and/or have a respiratory condition, such as asthma or COPD (Chronic Obstructive Pulmonary Disease).

If you give up smoking, you will save a significant amount of money.

This could be used to fund such things as an organic diet and/or a really good holiday!

BREATHE

ACTION

If you smoke - stop!
Use all the resources available to you from hypnotherapy to e-cigarettes, the latter temporarily.

Nicotine is a relaxant, so you need to find alternative ways to relax. Meditation, relaxation tapes and walking in nature can all help. Exercise helps to suppress nicotine cravings.

Plan what you will do with the money saved when you give up, and keep it in a separate and safe place to help with motivation.

If you have any respiratory problems, try using salt therapy to improve your condition.

BREATHE

If you are trying to improve your health, stopping smoking is so fundamental that it should be the first thing to be tackled.

Polluting your own air space is definitely not the wisest choice.

You can survive much longer without food and water but the significance of breathing is pretty well summed up with the following timescales as to what happens to your brain without oxygen (according to the University of Michigan Transplant Center).

After 1 minute without oxygen, brain cells begin to die but recovery is possible.

After 3 minutes without oxygen you will have serious brain injury.

After 10 minutes without oxygen so many brain cells will have died, recovery is unlikely

After 15 minutes without oxygen recovery is almost impossible.

When you are young, it's hard to imagine what it would be like to die of a smoking related disease, but one thing is certain, and well documented; smoking will definitely foreshorten your life even if it doesn't actually kill you directly from something like lung cancer, and it will age you prematurely!

Of course, it's possible to have lung problems through no fault of your own, and alongside medication, there are things that you can do to improve lung function.

If you are overweight, losing weight will help with lung capacity, and eating a good diet will improve immunity and reduce the risk of respiratory infection. Exercise should also improve lung capacity, but going outside in cold damp air is likely to make things worse. In fact, moving to a warm dry climate is likely to cause significant improvement, but may not be a practical solution for the majority.

Living in a polluted city is going to cause more lung problems than in the purer air of the countryside, although seasonal pollen can affect breathing in both town and country.

A salt pipe allows you to breathe in air that passes through salt before reaching your lungs, and may help provide relief. Sleeping in a room with a salt lamp switched on could also be beneficial.

Salt pipes and lamps offer the natural benefits of salt mine therapy by recreating the microclimate of a therapeutic salt mine, cleaning the respiratory system to flush out impurities and improve the overall health of all areas involved in breathing. This clinically proven therapy can help to improve symptoms for sufferers of asthma, allergies, bronchitis, colds, COPD (Chronic Obstructive Pulmonary Disease), emphysema, respiratory problems caused by smoking, rhinitis, snoring and whooping cough.

Treatment is simple: you breathe in through the device and out through the nose for 15 minutes per day.

When you breathe in, the moisture of the passing air absorbs tiny particles of salt as it passes through the central chamber. These micron sized particles of salt cleanse the respiratory system as they pass through, before being breathed out through the nose.

The treatment also boosts the body's natural self-cleansing mechanisms to further help rid the respiratory system of impurities and ease irritation caused by allergies and infection. This drug-free treatment may offer an alternative to steroid treatments typically prescribed for chronic breathing disorders whilst also boosting overall respiratory health to protect against acute conditions, such as coughs and chest infections.

Having a salt lamp switched on in the bedroom and/or living areas can be used alongside a salt pipe to enhance the effect, or may be used alone.

Salt caves

For a more intense experience, there are now man-made salt caves in several areas in the UK. Salt Therapy aka Halotherapy is a powerful, natural treatment in a controlled air medium that simulates the natural salt cave microclimate to treat respiratory and skin conditions. It has been shown to reduce the need for inhalers and antibiotics, improve lung function, reduce the number of hospital admissions, alleviates coughing, sneezing and shortness of breath and helps to clear mucous from the lungs. The immune system is strengthened and resistance to respiratory tract infections is increased, and remission times prolonged. The efficacy of halotherapy is estimated at 75-98%, depending on the condition. It also improves general health overall and can enhance sport performance.

In the UK the Salt Cave state that the NHS officially endorses Salt Therapy to treat COPD (Chronic Obstructive Pulmonary Disease) and that in clinical trials Salt Therapy proved to be effective in relieving symptoms of a variety of respiratory and skin ailments. During one of these trials, Salt Therapy was said to have resulted in improvement of the clinical state in:

- 85% of mild and moderate asthma cases
- 75% of severe asthma cases
- 97% of chronic bronchitis, bronchiectasis and cystic fibrosis cases

Studies relating to halotherapy can be found at: http://saltcave.co.uk/adults/list-of-studies

The salt caves in Poland are the most intense and effective of the salt therapies available. The Wieliczka Salt Mine in Poland offers treatments in the underground mining chambers using the unique micro-climate. The air in the caves is free of pollution and allergens, rich in micronutrients, with a constant temperature, high humidity, and free from harmful radiation.

This innovative treatment method, known as "subterranotherapy", was created at the mine, and active rehabilitation of the respiratory system is still conducted there, using the medicinal properties of the underground environment.

Airnergy

There is also a device called Airnergy, which is a portable, compact machine that creates 'energised air' following the principle of photosynthesis. This allows blood to carry more oxygen and cells to utilise oxygen more efficiently. Energy levels are increased, and concentration improved. The immune system is strengthened, the cardiovascular system and lungs are stimulated and stress levels improved. Discussed on the UK TV "This Morning" show, Dr Chris Steele said:

"Airnergy boosts antioxidants, taking away free radicals (a high level of free radicals is a common denominator in most diseases) … certainly could help patients with M.E. and any degenerative disease like macular degeneration, arthritis and heart disease …"

It has been shown to increase Peak Flow in asthma sufferers and the device is used by the German Olympic team.

BREATHE

RESOURCES

Books

Water and Salt: The Essence of Life

Barbara Hendel; Peter Ferreira. Nov 2003

ISBN-13: 978-0974451510

Water and Salt: Your Healers from within

F. Batmanhelidj; September 2003

ISBN-13: 978-1903571248

Stop Smoking: Hypnotherapy

Quit Smoking Today Without Gaining Weight

Paul McKenna. 2007 (Book and CD)

ISBN-13: 978-0593055366

Stop Smoking: Emotional Freedom Technique (EFT: aka "tapping")

Gary Craig, Stanford trained scientist and founder of Emotional Freedom Techniques (EFT) explains that, *"conventional smoking cessation systems don't work because they do not address the real reason that people smoke which is to tranquilize emotional issues like anxiety or low self esteem."*
A free series of EFT videos is available here and includes stop smoking:
http://www.tapping.com/videos.html

NHS Stop Smoking Service

In the UK the NHS (National Health Service) has a Stop Smoking service. Your GP (General

Practitioner) can provide help and advice about quitting, and refer you to an NHS Stop Smoking service, who state that you're four times more likely to quit smoking if you do it through the NHS. You can also make an appointment without seeing your doctor, by calling the NHS Stop Smoking helpline on 0300 123 1044 (England only).

There are several different stop smoking treatments, including:

Nicotine replacement therapy (NRT)

After smoking for a while your body adapts to getting regular doses of nicotine from your cigarettes. When you stop smoking you quickly remove the nicotine in your body, which means that you may experience withdrawal symptoms.

NRT comes in different forms including: skin patches, chewing gum, inhalers, tablets, strips and lozenges, which you put under your tongue, nasal spray and mouth spray. They can be prescribed by your GP or bought from a pharmacy.

Possible side effects of NRT include skin irritation when using patches, throat, nasal or eye irritation when using a nasal spray, disturbed sleep, sometimes with vivid dreams, upset stomach, dizziness or headaches.

Most courses of NRT last eight to twelve weeks before you gradually reduce the dose and eventually stop. Most people stop using NRT altogether within three months.

There are also two prescribed medications available:

Zyban (Buproprion) and Champix (Varenicline). Zyban (Buproprion) is used to help people who are addicted to nicotine to give up smoking. It acts in the brain but it isn't fully understood how the drug works to help people give up smoking. Bupropion affect neurotransmitters in the brain (chemicals stored in nerve cells involved in transmitting messages). It prevents two of these neurotransmitters, noradrenaline and dopamine, from being reabsorbed back into the nerve cells in the brain. Noradrenaline and dopamine are responsible for moderating mood and various other processes in the brain. It is thought that bupropion helps people to stop smoking by increasing the amount of noradrenaline and dopamine free to act in the brain, and is used in combination with motivational support techniques.

Champix (Varenicline) works by reducing the smoker's craving for nicotine by binding to nicotine receptors in the brain, which helps with the symptoms of withdrawal. It also reduces the satisfaction a smoker receives when smoking a cigarette.

More can be read about these drugs here:
http://www.nhs.uk/medicine-guides/pages/MedicineOverview.aspx?condition=Smoking%20Cessation&medicine=Zyban
http://www.champixinfo.co.uk

E-cigarettes

E-cigarettes (aka vaping) are not covered by the NHS and their safety is not yet proven. Electronic nicotine delivery systems (ENDS), of which electronic cigarettes are the most common prototype, are devices that do not burn or use tobacco leaves. Instead they vaporise a solution which is inhaled. Alongside nicotine (when nicotine is present), the solution contains propylene glycol (with or without glycerol and flavouring agents). ENDS solutions and emissions contain other chemicals, some of them considered to be toxicants.

The World Health Organization (WHO) is currently reviewing the existing evidence around Electronic Nicotine Delivery System (ENDS).

Salt inhalers and Lamps

Salt Therapies

Salt pipes and lamps are readily available online
Salt cave therapy is available at several locations:
e.g. http://ww.saltcave.co.uk
The Salt Mine in Poland: http://www.wieliczka-saltmine.com/health-resort/

Airnergy

Video about the Airnergy device which includes the This Morning TV interview with Dr Chris Steele:
http://airnergy-oxygen-therapy.co.uk/video.aspx

BUGS

BUGS

BENEFITS

Less inflammation.

Appetite normalises.

Reduced risk of obesity.

Less markers of metabolic syndrome: weight gain and insulin resistance.

BUGS

ACTION

Avoid all processed sugars.

Eat minimal sugar of any type.

Avoid all artificial sweeteners.

Sweeten food with unrefined stevia, coconut palm sugar and xylitol.

Eat prebiotics (i.e. what the good bugs live on) e.g. oats, unrefined barley, soybeans (non genetically modified), onions, garlic, leeks, chicory root, artichokes, asparagus and kiwi fruits.

Eat/drink probiotics (the source of the good bugs). Found in fermented foods: sauerkraut, kimchi, kefir, miso, cider apple vinegar, organic plain natural yogurt with probiotics (but not the highly sweetened dairy products with probiotics).

Or take a supplement e.g. Lactobacillus.

Exercise (any kind that's suitable for you personally).

BUGS

Our very existence may be completely different than we imagine according to Neil de Grasse Tyson: *"if you're one of the 100 billion bacteria living and working in a single centimeter of our lower intestine (rivaling, by the way, the total number of humans who have ever been born) you would give an entirely different answer. You might instead say that the purpose of human life is to provide you with a dark, but idyllic, anaerobic habitat of fecal matter."*

The human microbiome consists of more than 100 trillion microorganisms that live in our gut, mouth, skin and elsewhere in our bodies. These microbial communities have many beneficial functions relevant to supporting life: digesting food, preventing pathogens from invading the body; and synthesizing essential nutrients and vitamins.

The total number of genes associated with the human microbiome is greater than the total number of human genes by 100:1

http://genome.wustl.edu/projects/detail/human-microbiome-project/

The human microbiome is a fundamental part of human physiology and changes in the microbiome can cause changes to cellular activities resulting in disease or contributing to its progression.

Part of the human microbiome, there are billions and billions of bacteria in our intestines alone that have an effect on our general health and our weight. It's a combination of what you eat and exercise that keeps your intestinal bacteria in good shape, which both keeps you healthy and at a healthy weight.

It's pretty obvious that what we eat will influence what kind of bugs inhabit us, but its less obvious that exercise has a beneficial effect on these bacteria – another good reason to exercise!

But why should we care about our intestinal bacteria! Well, a healthy and varied gut bacteria ecosystem has been linked to everything from low obesity rates to fewer symptoms of mental disorders. And low diversity of gut bacteria is associated with inflammation and markers of metabolic syndrome such as weight gain and insulin resistance. New evidence indicates that intestinal bacteria alter the way we store fat, how we balance levels of glucose in the blood, and how we respond to hormones that make us feel hungry or full. It's believed that the bacteria within may predispose us from birth to obesity and diabetes.

But all is not lost! Not only can you alter your gut bacteria by eating natural foods containing probiotics and prebiotics, you can also affect the balance of bacteria through exercise! Already known to be good for heart health, muscle strengthening, fat loss and hormonal balance, it's now believed that exercise (at any level) can benefit intestinal bacteria, and that exercise and diet together can have a beneficial effect on the diversity of gut bacteria, metabolic profile and inflammation.

So, what if it goes wrong and you end up with a gut full of bad bacteria?

It could be a long-standing problem from before the weight gain started, and might be the fundamental reason for the weight gain in the first place! Perhaps prescribed antibiotics, which tended to be over-prescribed in the past, may have upset the balance of intestinal flora; i.e the good bugs v. the bad bugs!
Or poor lifestyle habits and food choices could be the reason.

So how to get the balance of bugs back to normal?
Prebiotics, Probiotics and reduction of inflammation.
Cutting out processed sugars and replacing with healthy alternatives is the first thing to start with, whilst keeping the use of all sugars low.
Processed sugars provide a breeding ground for

the bad bugs (and processed food also has an impact on weight gain for hormonal reasons).

NB Don't be tempted to replace refined sugar with artificial sweeteners or you're straight out of the frying pan and into the fire as these toxic substances give you a whole new set of problems, including weight gain!

Whenever possible find alternatives to these types of packaged foods and sweeten your foods with healthier sugars, like stevia, coconut palm sugar and xylitol.

Prebiotics are what the good bugs live on and are non-digestible food ingredients that work on the gut by inducing the growth of good bacteria. Prebiotics can be carbohydrates, soluble fibres or dietary fibres. They are present in various plants, particularly those rich in fructan e.g. kiwi fruit, asparagus, leeks, artichoke, garlic and onion. The vegetables are best raw or cooked very lightly. Soybeans (non genetically modified) are also good sources of prebiotics, and so are oats, unrefined barley and wheat and plants rich in inulin such as chicory root.

Probiotics are the source of the good bugs and are in fermented foods such as sauerkraut, kimchi, kefir and miso. You can also take a supplement to start to help the gut to heal. Organic plain natural yogurt with probiotics is also useful, but beware of highly sweetened dairy products with probiotics.

BUGS

RESOURCES

The Human Microbiome Project
http://genome.wustl.edu/projects/detail/human-microbiome-project/

Organic vegetables and fruit are available from:
vegetable box delivery services
farmers' markets
good supermarkets
online

Organic grains are available from:
health food stores
good supermarkets
online

Fermented foods are available from:
health food stores
good supermarkets
online

Some fermented food can be homemade.
Recipes can be found online for:
Sauerkraut; kimchi; kefir; cider apple vinegar

DIET

(NB in this context "Diet" refers to "dieting" as in weight loss)

For everyone, including those who are of normal weight, underweight or overweight at any level, a diet of fresh home-produced foods, avoiding processed food, is key to good health! Along with appropriate portion size and adequate exercise, taking into account age and physical condition.

Plus plenty of water, fresh air and enough sunlight, sleep, and stress control methods as necessary.

DIET

BENEFITS

Daily Calorie Restriction: Not recommended!

Daily calorie restriction can result in up to 25% muscle loss unless great care is taken to build muscle via adequate exercise. If lean tissue is lost, it tends to be replaced with fat, leaving you fatter and flabbier than before you dieted. Further rebound dieting continues to make the situation worse!

Any exposure to daily calorie restriction can result in a state called adaptive thermogenesis. You then need considerably fewer calories, possibly for the rest of your life!

This includes all forms of daily calorie restriction diets.

Intermittent Fasting: Recommended

Modified Alternate Day Fasting
5:2 Diet

This form of fasting does not result in any muscle loss if exercising, and only 5% of loss of lean tissue without exercise.
Does not result in rebound dieting
May be less effective if there is a history of daily calorie restriction

DIET

ACTION

Don't use Daily Calorie Restriction to attempt to lose weight!
If it worked, we would not have the obesity crisis that we have today
You are likely to end up fatter and flabbier than when you started!

Do consider using Intermittent Fasting to lose weight.
Modified Alternate Day Fasting has been proven to work via clinical trials.
The 5:2 Diet is also effective for some people, but does not have the clinical research to prove it.
There are 10% for whom even Modified Alternate Day fasting doesn't work. To get results they have to also restrict calories on non-fast days.

Juice Fasting may be effective for weight control and appears to allow the skin to be more flexible and return to it's former shape without the need for surgery. Plant proteins and adequate exercise should mitigate against muscle loss.

Hypnotherapy is an effective alternative to dieting for weight loss.

DIET

(NB in this context "Diet" refers to "dieting" as in weight loss)

There are gazillions of weight loss diets out in the big wide world.

Yet they can all be categorised into 2 major types:

Daily Calorie Restriction

and

Intermittent Fasting

If you restrict calories enough, everyone will lose weight eventually. We have enough human tragedy throughout the aeons to confirm this to be true. It is what happens to your body whilst you are restricting calories and the effects afterwards that cause the problems.

There are 3 reasons why daily calorie restriction causes these problems:

- Your body's metabolism resets itself, so that you burn less calories, usually for the rest of your life. You need 15-25% fewer calories and if you return to your pre-diet calorie intake, you will inevitably gain weight. This is called "adaptive thermogenesis".
- During conventional daily calorie restriction dieting, you lose muscle along with fat. 75% fat and 25% muscle. Muscle is metabolically active and burns calories faster. Weight regained is usually fat.
- Your hormones related to hunger alter. You make more ghrelin, the hormone that makes you hungry and less leptin, the

hormone that decreases hunger. With increased hunger, you inevitably eat more.

The Every Other Day Diet: Krista Varady; Bill Gottlieb. Pub: Jan 2014

"Dieting" is a billion dollar industry, and I'd like you to entertain the thought that there are people and organisations out there who have a vested interest in you not losing weight permanently! From a business perspective, retaining a customer is easier than acquiring a new one. If you were to lose weight permanently, you are then lost forever to this billion dollar industry. An ideal "dieting" customer is one who loses weight, puts it all back on and possibly more. And thinks that the fault lies solely with themselves.

Up-selling products to this rebounding customer is the icing on the highly processed cake! There will always be a small percentage for whom any diet is effective, and it is this small percentage that give some level of dubious credibility to the industry. Getting hold of the figures is tricky and their lack of availability may give reason to believe that the very low levels of long term success are kept very quiet!

> *"Diets don't work when you diet every day!"*
> Dr Krista Varady

However, with intermittent fasting, there's a new kid on the block!
And one that has been thoroughly clinically researched by Dr Krista Varady, who has had high levels of long term weight control success

documented in clinical trials via her modified alternate day fasting.

Dr Michael Moseley then went on to success with his 5:2 diet.

Although less restrictive than alternate day fasting, and anecdotally proven to be successful, it does not have clinical research to back it up.

Both of these diets have days where you eat to appetite, and days where you restrict calorie intake to 500 for women and 600 for men.

For alternate day fasting, you fast for four days one week and three days alternate weeks. alternating daily between fasting and normal healthy eating. Intermittent fasting doesn't have the same problems with muscle loss as conventional dieting, there appear to be no problems with either adaptive thermogenesis or the hormones related to hunger.

According to Varady, there are about 10% of people for whom alternate day fasting is unsuccessful. To be effective the diet can then be modified by reducing the calorie intake to 1500 on the non-fasting days.

For the 5:2 diet, you only restrict calories for two days each week.

As a postmenopausal woman with a past history of daily calorie restriction, the only way I was able to lose any weight with intermittent fasting was to restrict calories on the non-fast days to 1500.

With this modification in place, over 12 weeks I lost a total of 12 lb (5.5 kg). However, I have personally observed several people lose a considerable amount of weight, simply by following the 5:2 diet.

DIET

(NB in this context "Diet" refers to "dieting" as in weight loss)

RESOURCES

The Every Other Day Diet: Krista Varady; Bill Gottlieb
Pub: Jan 2014
ISBN-10: 1444780123
ISBN-13: 978-1444780123

The Fast Diet: The Secret of Intermittent Fasting - Lose Weight, Stay Healthy, Live Longer: Dr Michael Mosley; Mimi Spencer
Pub: Jan 2013
ISBN-10: 1780721676
ISBN-13: 978-1780721675

I Can Make You Thin - Love Food, Lose Weight: Paul McKenna
Pub: Jan 2010 (Book + CD and DVD)
ISBN-10: 0593064437
ISBN-13: 978-0593064436

Freedom from Emotional Eating: Paul McKenna
Pub: Jan 2014(Book + CD + DVD)
ISBN-10: 0593064070
ISBN-13: 978-0593064078

DETOX

DETOX

BENEFITS

For best results follow all three practices

below:

Salt Therapy:

Dr Barbara Hendel claims that a 30 minute soak in a bath filled with 1 Kilo of Himalayan Salt has the same detoxing effect as a three day fast in her book: Salt & Water.

Juice Fasting:

Rests and repairs the whole gastrointestinal tract.
Rests the liver.
Reduces appetite.
Maximises nutrition.
Increases energy
Heals at a cellular level.

Skin brushing:

Stimulates your lymphatic system.
Improves your circulation.
Exfoliates your skin.
May reduce cellulite.
Reduces stress.
Is invigorating.

DETOX ACTION

For best results follow all three practices below:

Detox: Salt Therapy

Use 3 times per week for 2 weeks, then when needed.

Dissolve 500g -1K Himalayan pink salt in a regular bath at about 37C.

Relax and soak for about 20 minutes or so.

For general well being use approx 100g-200g per regular sized bath.

Detox: Juice Fasting: see the chapter entitled FAST

Prepare for a fast by making changes several days beforehand

e.g. reduce then remove caffeine and animal products.

Fast on juiced vegetables, not water, and use organic produce.

Plan the fast for a time when it is easiest for you to do it.

It is usually easier to fast when the weather is warm and pleasant rather than in the depths of winter.

Break the fast carefully, by introducing raw vegetables and fruit then salads and vegetarian soups and stews.

Juice Fasting holidays are popular as it's easier when in a group.

Detox: Skin Brushing

Skin brush daily for about 5 minutes, ideally in the morning.

Using a dry skin brush with firm natural bristles, sweep towards your heart.

Use gentle pressure and long sweeping strokes (after brushing, skin should be pink rather than red).

Shower after dry skin brushing, ideally alternating from warm to cold.

DETOX

Conventional medicine doesn't consider detoxification (detox) necessary as can be seen by the following quote from the NHS Live Well website, which also appears to make the presumption that "detox" is simply related to trying to lose weight.

"Detox diets are based on the idea that toxins build up in the body and can be removed by eating, or not eating, certain things. However, there's no evidence that toxins build up in our bodies. If they did, we would feel very ill."

I totally agree with this statement if the diet eaten is minimally processed foods, organically grown and eaten raw or home cooked, along with pure and unpolluted air and water. But as far back as the 1960's, persistent toxic compounds (PTC's) were found in Antarctica. According to a study published in 2002, undertaken by The United Nations Environment Programme: "This assessment of persistent toxic substances (PTS's) in Antarctica forms part of a regionally-based global assessment. The Antarctic has been important in highlighting the pervasive nature of anthropogenic pollution. The discovery of DDT-related compounds in Antarctic biota in the 1960s and in the environment in the 1970s was a clear and well publicised indication of the global impact of human activities".

http://www.chem.unep.ch/pts/regreports/Antarctica%20full%20report.pdf

The long term results on health of PTC's found in humans are not yet known.

According to Scientific American in 2011, mercury in fish for human consumption is a big problem throughout the world. Although mercury is a naturally occurring element, present throughout the environment and in plants and animals, human industrial activity (e.g. coal-fired electricity generation, smelting and incineration of waste) increases the amount of airborne mercury which eventually reaches lakes, rivers and the ocean, where it is inadvertently eaten by fish and other marine life.

Once this mercury gets into the marine food chain, it "bioaccumulates" in the larger predators. One of these larger predators is tuna, which are then eaten by us, and we therefore also ingest mercury.

Mercury bioaccumulates in tuna.

Tuna eat a completely natural diet and lead a completely natural lifestyle. As mercury also bioaccumulates in us via the tuna we eat, it would seem advisable to use natural methods to try to remove this persistent toxic substance from our bodies, along with any other persistent toxic substances inadvertently ingested, inhaled or absorbed.

Another group of substances known to be toxic are phthalates, which are found in plastics Phthalates disrupt hormones, may cause birth defects and may cause cancer. They are found in some plastic toys, some personal care products, and some plastic food containers, with the single largest source of phthalate exposure coming from our food and water supply. Almost all of us have phthalates in our systems, and the recent study below showed that when fasting, people's phthalate levels dropped by five to ten times within the first 24 hours without food.

Int J Hyg Environ Health. 2013 Nov;216(6):672-81. doi: 10.1016/j.ijheh.2012.12.002. Epub 2013 Jan 18.

Identifying sources of phthalate exposure with human biomonitoring: results of a 48h fasting study with urine collection and personal activity patterns.

Koch HM[1], Lorber M, Christensen KL, Pälmke **C***, Koslitz S, Brüning T.*

It would seem that our bodies are not as good at eliminating toxins as conventional medicine would have us believe!

There are four basic routes of elimination: the colon (i.e. the bowels or large intestine, with faeces as the end-product), the lungs (air/breath), kidneys (urine, via the bladder) and skin (via sweating).

Three simple methods of detoxification include

- Juice fasting
- Salt therapy (halotherapy)
- Skin brushing

Juice Fasting is discussed in the chapter entitled "Fast".

Salt therapy is discussed in the chapter entitled "Breathe", with further suggestions here in "Detox".

Skin brushing is contained within this chapter.

DETOX: Skin Brushing

Skin is a complex system made up of nerves, glands and layers of cells that, when healthy, help protect your body from extreme temperatures and chemicals. It produces antibacterial substances to protect from infection and enables your body to produce vitamin D when exposed to the sun. Skin also contains densely packed nerve cells, acting as messengers to your brain.

Another crucial role your skin plays is supporting optimal detoxification. But if your skin is overrun with toxins or dead skin cells, it will not be able to eliminate wastes from your body efficiently. Skin brushing not only removes dead skin cells, it also removes waste via the lymphatic system.

The lymphatic system is responsible for eliminating cellular waste products. Hundreds of miles of lymphatic tubules allow waste to be collected from your tissues in a process called lymphatic drainage.

If the lymphatic system is not working properly, waste and toxins can build up and cause illness. Lymphatic congestion is a major factor leading to inflammation and disease. Lymph is moved around the body when you move, and skin brushing is best practiced alongside exercise. Dry skin brushing is a powerful detoxification process and helps release toxins via the lymphatic system. It increases circulation which encourages the elimination of metabolic waste. It is simultaneously both relaxing and stimulating.

Also exfoliating, it removes dead skin, clears clogged pores and also
helps to soften hard fat deposits below the skin, while distributing fat deposits more evenly. This may help to diminish the appearance of cellulite. Dr Kitty Campion says that 5 minutes of energetic skin brushing is equivalents to 30 minutes jogging, as far as physical tone is concerned, and that it will build up healthy muscle tone and stimulate better distribution of fat deposits. Overall it may help you to feel younger and
gives a feeling of well being.

You skin brush using a long-handled natural bristle brush and these are readily available from chemists, department stores, health food shops and online. It must be a natural bristle brush to obtain the benefits of skin brushing. A good time to skin brush is before a morning shower, and ideally you would have a shower alternative the temperature from warm to cold. Skin brushing at night isn't recommended as it might wake you up.

Brush towards your heart, which is best for circulation and your lymphatic system, and brush your entire body (including the soles of your feet). Start at your feet and work your way up your legs to your arms, chest, back, and stomach. Avoid brushing your face (unless you have a special brush designed for this delicate skin), other delicate areas i.e. nipples and genitals, or if there are any irritations or abrasions (including varicose veins).

The pressure you apply while brushing your skin should be firm but not painful, and should be long sweeping strokes, upwards towards the heat and downwards towards the heart.

Practice dry skin brushing daily for the greatest benefits.

DRINK

DRINK

BENEFITS

Water helps with weight loss.

Water helps with headaches and dizziness.

Water helps to fight infections.

Water helps with exercise.

Water improves concentration.

Water improves energy levels.

Water reduces the risk of heart attacks and strokes.

DRINK

ACTION

Drink 2 Litres of water daily.
Herbal teas and freshly pressed vegetable juices can be substituted, but not tea or coffee (plus a single serving of freshly pressed fruit juice).

Adjust fluid intake to take into account exercise and climate.

Drink tea and coffee in moderation.

Avoid sodas because of high levels of sugar or artificial sweeteners. Substitute with sparkling water and a squeeze of lime or lemon.

Drink water on rising to help with elimination.

Drink water before going to bed to help avoid heart attacks and stroke.

Drink water throughout the day to keep hydrated.

Drink water throughout the day to suppress appetite to help with weight loss.

Keep alcohol intake within recommended guidelines or less.

DRINK

UK government guidelines advise drinking at least 1.5 Litres / eight glasses daily to stay hydrated.

Chronic dehydration has many effects on your health and your life.

Water can help with weight loss as your brain can tell you are hungry when you are actually thirsty. When you're dehydrated, fat cells become harder to break down, so weight loss is easier if you drink enough.

Dehydration can cause headaches and dizziness. Plus tension headaches and dizziness brought on by fatigue can be helped by drinking water, as fatigue is also a sign of dehydration.

Drinking more water helps to clear skin, including acne symptoms.

For dry skin, drinking water will give it more moisture, and water flushes toxins out of your body, helping to clear skin.

Drinking water can help fight infections all over your body, not only because it flushes out toxins, but also because when you're dehydrated you are more vulnerable to infection.

Water is especially good for getting rid of and preventing urine infections, although if you already have a urine infection drinking cranberry juice will also help. This is because cranberry juice affects the cell wall of the urinary tract.

Drinking water also helps with colds and allergies because it clears the airways. And even cold sores can be reduced by drinking more water because they can occur where your skin is particularly dry.

If you suffer from constipation or haemorrhoids, besides eating more fibre, you need to drink more water for the fibre to work properly. More fibre without water could exacerbate the problem.

You can exercise more efficiently if you drink water, and you also need to replace the fluids lost through sweating after exercise.

Both concentration and short-term memory can be affected by dehydration. As well as the brain, dehydration affects the body, causing tiredness and low energy.

Blood gets thicker if you are dehydrated, making your heart work harder, and drinking more than five glasses of water a day reduces the risk of heart attack by 41%, compared with people who drank less than two glasses. Drinking water before bed reduces risk of heart attack and stroke during the night.

Institute of Medicine. Dietary Reference Intakes: Water, Potassium, Sodium, Chloride, and Sulfate. February 11, 2004.
Water, Other Fluids, and Fatal Coronary Heart Disease: The Adventist Study. American Journal of Epidemiology 2002 May;155(9):827-833.

Although UK government guidelines say that we should all drink 8 glasses of water daily; height, weight and the size of the glass can all make a difference.

The average amount of urine passed daily is about 1.5 L and fluid lost via breathing and sweating is about 1 L.

About 20% of our fluid intake comes from the food we eat, making 2 L about right for most people.

The 2 L recommended includes water, herbal teas (unless a diuretic tea) and freshly pressed juices. Coffee and tea, being diuretics, are best not counted in the 2 L.

Exercise, climate, illness, pregnancy and breastfeeding all affect fluid requirements and you need to take these into consideration and adjust fluid intake accordingly.

Tea and coffee are diuretics, which make you pass more water, so are best used in small quantities. Sodas contain either large amounts of sugar or artificial sweeteners and are best avoided!

When you think you're hungry, drink water first as you may just be thirsty!

Start the day with 2 big glasses of water (perhaps with the juice of half a lemon).

Have another big glass of water before each meal and up to four more glasses in-between meals or in the evening.

Using a water filter is thought to be the best way to drink tap water, using either a jug with a filter or having a filter system attached to the water supply.

Some of the water can be substituted for herbal teas (green, chamomile, rooibos, mint, fruit etc). The water helps you to feel full, hydrates the skin and keeps your digestive system working well.

Along with the water you could drink as much freshly pressed vegetable juice as you like. But fruit juice, even freshly pressed, tends to spike your blood sugar levels, so is best kept to a minimum.

Far better to eat the whole fruit!

Pasteurised juice in cartons and bottles is best avoided altogether. Because pasteurisation has effectively "cooked" the juice, the health-giving properties are lost and it also contains too much fructose.

If you are a tea or coffee drinker, the best time to have a cup of freshly brewed coffee or tea is in the morning after exercising.

Instant coffee and soft drinks are best kept to a minimum.

If you want a fizzy drink, sparkling water with a twist of lemon or lime is a good alternative to soft drinks.

Did you know that licensed establishments (those that serve alcohol) in England, Wales and Scotland must provide free drinking water? According to Section 136 of the Licensing Act 2003, which came into force in April 2010, all restaurants in England and Wales that serve alcohol are legally required to give customers free tap water (it's the same legislation for Scotland, but a different act).

The maximum penalty for breaching a license condition in England and Wales is six months in prison and/or a fine of up to £20,000. But it's more likely to prompt a review by the licensing authority, which could result in the establishment losing their license to sell alcohol.

Although all licensed restaurants, bars, clubs and cafes are legally obliged to provide tap water free of charge, they can charge for the use of the glass or service, but rarely do so in practice.

And then there's alcohol…..

So, what's your poison?

"Eat, drink and be merry, for tomorrow we die"

Everyone has their "thing"!

For me it's not alcohol, it's chocolate!

In moderation both alcohol and chocolate have health benefits…..with moderation being the key!

With alcohol you have a triple whammy with regard to weight gain:

- Alcohol is empty calories
- Alcohol stimulates the appetite
- Alcohol removes inhibitions

It's soooo easy to take in extra calories by drinking them! But, on the plus side, it's usually much easier to lose weight if you stop drinking. Then with your appetite stimulated it's soooo easy to eat more as well!

With the resolve to eat less diminished by the alcohol, and with overeating more likely last thing at night when you get back from a drinking session (and again in the morning when you need a substantial breakfast to get over a hangover), you have a perfect scenario for alcohol related weight gain! Not to mention the risks to your health!

According to the NHS, alcohol-related health problems may only occur after a number of years, by which time serious health problems may have developed.

Liver problems, reduced fertility, high blood pressure, increased risk of various cancers and heart attack are some of the harmful effects of regularly drinking more than the recommended levels, with the effects of alcohol on your health directly related to how much you drink.

But how much is too much alcohol?

Units are how the alcohol content in alcoholic drinks is measured. This is a simpler way of representing alcohol content, which is usually expressed by the standard measure ABV, which stands for alcohol by volume.

ABV is a measure of the amount of pure alcohol as a percentage of the total volume of liquid in a drink.

You can find the ABV on the labels of cans and bottles, sometimes written as "vol" or "alcohol volume" or you can ask bar staff about particular drinks.

For example, wine that says "12% ABV" or "alcohol volume 12%" means that 12% of the volume of that drink is pure alcohol.

You can work out how many units there are in any drink by multiplying the total volume of a drink (in mls) by its ABV (which is measured as a percentage) and dividing the result by 1,000.

Strength (ABV) x Volume (ml) ÷ 1,000 = units

So how much is the recommended amount of alcohol to keep you in the lower risk category? UK government guidelines suggest the following:

- For women the maximum amount is 2 to 3 units of alcohol daily
- For men the maximum amount is 3 to 4 units of alcohol daily

Doing the maths to work out units is probably best done by downloading an app on your phone (or see below).

Or work out in advance the units of your regular drinks and then take care to keep track.

Here's a list of the amount of units in a selection of drinks – but that's if you actually measure them! Easy when you are out in a bar or restaurant, but an entirely different kettle of fish if you are pouring your own at home!

- 1 unit: Single shot of spirits (e.g. gin, whisky, vodka, brandy) 25mls ABV 40%
- 1.4 units: Large single measure of spirits: 35mls ABV 40%
- 1.5 units: Alcopops: 275mls ABV 5.5%
- 1.5 units: Small glass of wine (red, white, rose): 125mls ABV 12%
- 1.7 units: Bottle of beer, cider, lager: 330mls ABV 5%
- 2 units: Pint of beer, cider, lager: ABV 3.6%

- 2 units: Can of beer, lager, cider: 440mls ABV 4.5%
- 2.1 units: Standard glass of wine (red, white, rose): 175mls ABV 12%
- 3 units: Pint of higher strength beer, cider, lager: ABV 5.2%
- 3 units: Large glass of wine (red, white, rose): 250mls ABV 12%
- 10 units: Bottle of wine: 750mls ABV 13.5%

The maths:

Units are just a way of showing the quantity of pure alcohol in a drink. One unit equals 10 ml or 8 g of pure alcohol, which is around the amount of alcohol an average adult can process in an hour i.e. theoretically, within an hour, there should be little or no alcohol left in the blood of an adult (but this may vary from person to person).

The number of units in a drink is based on the size of the drink as well as its alcohol strength e.g. a pint of strong lager contains 3 units of alcohol and standard lager has just over 2 unit

DRINK

RESOURCES

Books

Your Body's Many Cries for Water: You're Not Sick, You're Thirsty: Don't Treat Thirst with Medications

F.Batmanghelidj

Pub. September 2008

ISBN-13: 978-0970245885

The True Power of Water: Healing and Discovering Ourselves

Masaru Emoto

Pub. December 2005

ISBN-13: 978-1416522171

Water filtration systems, ranging from simple jugs to whole house systems, are readily available online

Herbal teas are available in supermarkets, health food shops and online

Juicers are available both in department stores and online. Read reviews to decide which type would suit you best i.e. masticating or centrifugal.

EARTH

EARTH

BENEFITS

Improves the symptoms of some inflammation-related disorders by defusing the cause of the inflammation.

Reduces chronic pain.

Improves sleep.

Increases energy.

Reduces stress levels.

May improve blood pressure by thinning the blood and improving flow.

Relieves muscular tension and headaches.

Reduces hormonal and menstrual symptoms.

Speeds healing.

Reduces jet lag.

EARTH

ACTION

Go outdoors in unspoilt and unpolluted areas.

Go barefoot outdoors in nature as often as possible.

Swim in the ocean, lakes and rivers.

Wear shoes with leather soles or ESD (Electro Static Discharge) Grounding shoes.

Use a Car Grounding Pad and/or a Vehicle Grounding Strip on your car that connects your car with the ground below.

Use a barefoot substitute i.e. a conductive material that 'connects' your body to the earth e.g. mats; pads; sheets.

EARTH

Do you feel better when you walk barefoot on the beach or across a new mown lawn in the garden?

Grounding / Earthing has to be one of the simplest solutions to improving health.

"Earthing restores and maintains the human body's most natural electrical state, which in turn promotes natural health and functionality in daily life. The primordial natural energy emanating from the Earth is the ultimate anti-inflammatory and the ultimate anti-aging medicine."

James L. Oschman, Ph.D

The known effect of grounding is that it discharges and prevents the build-up of electrical stress. This knowledge is used in the Electro-Static Discharge (ESD) business in the UK as a form of safety and one of reducing (grounding) voltage (Static Electricity) levels in the human body to protect both humans and sensitive electronic equipment.

A modern lifestyle prevents most people from spending time in direct contact with the earth. But we evolved over aeons in direct contact with the earth, walking barefoot and sleeping on the earth and using shoes made of natural materials. All of this kept us 'grounded' aka 'earthed'. Nowadays we wear shoes with rubber soles that insulate us from contact with the Earth, and sleep in beds away from connection with the Earth.

In the mid-1900s in the UK we switched our electricity supply from Direct Current (DC) to Alternating Current (AC). With this change came the Electric and Electromagnetic fields that may be affecting our health nowadays. Alongside this are mobile phone masts and wireless gizmos. It's believed that we are affected by electrical radiation which can lead to a build-up of electrical stress. Electrosensitivity (ES) is a known and recognised medical condition in Sweden.

Chronic conditions are increasing and it may be that electrical radiation has a part to play in this. A direct conductive connection with the Earth lets us experience the connection with the Earth's essential energy field. When your body is earthed it becomes a conductor as well as an antenna and can now discharge any extra voltage from the body.

EARTH

RESOURCES

http://www.geoharmony.co.uk Audio book and pdf: free to download Earthing: The Most Important Health Discovery Ever?

Clinton Ober, Stephen T. Sinatra, M.D., Martin Zucker

Earthing: The Most Important Health Discovery Ever?

Clinton Ober, Stephen T. Sinatra, M.D., Martin Zucker

Pub. April 2010

ISBN-13: 978-1591202837

Earthing products are readily available online, including http://www.geoharmony.co.uk e.g. mats; pads; sheets; vehicle grounding equipment.

EAT

"Let food be thy medicine, and medicine be thy food"
Hippocrates

EAT

BENEFITS

Normalise Body Weight.

Increase Energy.

Clear Skin.

Improve Hair.

Better Sleep.

Increase physical and mental wellbeing.

EAT

ACTION

Stay well hydrated.
(see DRINK)

Avoid all processed food.

Eat organic produce whenever possible.

Increase vegetables and fruit intake.

Reduce sugar to a minimum.

Eat healthy fats:
virgin cold-pressed olive oil, coconut oil, avocado, nuts and seeds.

Eat whole grains instead of refined.

Eat fermented foods to increase good bacteria in your microbiome:
sauerkraut, kim chi, miso, tempeh.

Learn to cook from scratch. Use online videos, online recipes, TV shows and recipe books.

Grow your own food if you are able to.

EAT

Human beings are adaptable and can experience excellent health and longevity on a variety of diets, so long as it is minimally processed. This needs to be alongside appropriate levels of physical activity, sleep, reduction in stress and a change in attitude towards lifestyle choices.

No matter where you live in the world, unless your environment makes this impossible through drought and famine or war, you can personally eat the best diet in the world by the choices you make! In wealthy countries, the choice has to be deliberate, as there are a plethora of unhealthy options. In many poor countries, choice is often limited, but processed food may be unknown, especially in rural areas.

Eating a diet that is as natural as possible, minimally processed, home cooked and prepared, and preferably organic, is likely to lead to the best possible health.

Conversely, a diet full of processed foods, full of chemicals, grown in depleted soil and sprayed with herbicides and pesticides is likely to lead to poor health.

All of my life, people have told me what I'm eating is wrong! Right from newborn when my Mum couldn't breast feed me because of a spinal problem. No-one's fault, but I suspect my health throughout my life would have been entirely different if I hadn't been fed formulas based on cow's milk. And when I couldn't tolerate them I was eventually fed the strangest of combinations for a new baby - evaporated milk watered down with barley water. This unlikely combination may have been the trigger for my intolerance to both dairy products and gluten!

It would also have affected my gut bacteria, although little would have been known about any of this back in 1951.

Much more recently we have learned about epigenetics, where assaults on the health of one generation can echo down for a further three generations!

My Mum was orphaned as a little girl out in Africa, and half starved for 7 years in a brutal orphanage. It's now known that periods of starvation are likely to have an impact on the health of up to three generations thereafter!

All through childhood, my natural inclination was towards a vegan diet, which I probably instinctively knew was the least likely to cause me harm. But everyone felt I should be eating meat….and dairy....and wheat….and I was very very unwell at times….

And so it went on! With everyone keen to advise, right through to recent times when I've been advised of the dangers of organic produce (honestly!) and simultaneously that I'm not organic enough! The juicers want me to juice more; the raw foodies want me to eat raw and cold, the macrobiotic dieter's want me to eat everything cooked; the vegetarians want me to give up meat and fish and the vegans want me to give up everything from the animal kingdom. The omnivores are unimpressed unless I'm eating everything in sight…..and as for the carnivores……!!!

I'm just grateful that I have never lived through famine and that I've finally worked out for myself what foods are detrimental!

And without this background, I may never have followed the path to find the secrets to good health that have been a quest throughout my life!

Eating around the globe:

A UK documentary "The World's Best Diet" was presented by Jimmy Doherty and Kate Quilton, who travelled around the world taking a look at shopping and eating habits across the globe, and the place with the very best diet might take you by surprise!

And there are a few much further down the list than perhaps expected……

1 Iceland!

I didn't see this one coming! It's believed to be a combination of the uniquely pure environment, a unique gene pool and an exceptionally good diet that puts the Icelandic people at the very top of the list!

Men in Iceland have the longest life expectancy in the whole world. They eat copious amounts of fresh wild fish, rich in Omega 3 fatty acids which are essential for the brain.

Their dairy products come from local farms with grass-fed animals, yielding milk rich in beta-carotene, known to be good for the immune system, eye health and the skin. And their bread is made from rye. Everything is produced on small family farms in one of the cleanest environments in the world.

2 & 3 Greece & Italy

The traditional Mediterranean diet is rich in olive oil, legumes, whole grain cereals, vegetables, fruit and fish, alongside moderate amounts of dairy products and red meat. The olive oil, when combined with salad and vegetables, lowers cholesterol and blood pressure and is also now believed to help prevent Alzheimer's disease. Many people in this region eat home grown and homemade food and the relaxed lifestyle is also influential.

4 Seventh Day Adventists

This religious group is a branch of Christianity. For spiritual reasons they don't drink or smoke, drink caffeine or eat red meat. Their diet is rich in fruit and vegetables, nuts, seeds and dried fruits.

It was said that research in the US shows that being a Seventh Day Adventist adds an extra ten years to your life!

5 Japan

With a diet rich in fish and vegetables, it could have been expected that Japan might have made it almost to the top of the list! But their high salt diet via soy sauce is linked to strokes, which is the 3rd leading cause of death in Japan. Plus the influence of Western cuisine has decreased the traditional consumption of fish and vegetables.

6 The Nordic Countries – Sweden, Norway, Denmark

The Nordic diet is rich in berries, fish, seasonal vegetables and whole grains such as oats and rye. This diet is being referred to as the Mediterranean diet of the North.

7 The Kuna Indians of Panama

Besides not eating processed foods, the Kuna Indians have a diet rich in cocoa, drinking up to 5 cups daily.

They have the lowest rates of cardiovascular disease and blood pressure problems in the world.

8 France

The French eat a diet rich in fat, meat and cheese and drink red wine, yet have low levels of cholesterol and heart disease! This phenomenon is known as "The French Paradox" But it's not just what they eat, it's an overall attitude to food that is fundamentally different.

The French eat 3 proper meals a day, eat small portions and don't snack! One of my favourite differences is that they believe that an hour for lunch is the minimum amount of time.

Along with the lifestyle differences, there's resveratrol in red wine, which is believed to have a beneficial effect on the cardiovascular system.

Researchers in Cambridge in the UK believe that the mould on blue cheeses such as Roquefort also has an anti-inflammatory effect on the cardiovascular system.

9 Spain

Women in Spain are the longest living in Europe, second only to Japan! Along with other Mediterranean countries, a diet rich in vegetables and fruit, fish and olive oil, along with a relaxed attitude, are contributory factors to Spanish longevity.

Many placing's are as you'd expect. The US scored low thanks to the consumption of high-fructose corn syrup, and over-consumption in general. Southern European countries with a Mediterranean diet did well. But there were also surprises and tragedies, particularly the place with the very worst diet! A man-made tragedy completely out of the control of the indigenous population!

Counting down to the Very Worst Diet in the World:

8 The USA

Surprisingly, the US has seven global diets below it, but with the exception of Russia, its influence has been pervasive!

"Fast Food" in the US began with political decisions. In 1971 the high cost of food had President Nixon worried about re-election and he introduced the mass production of crops, including corn. Excess corn was made into HFCS (High Fructose Corn Syrup) which is used in processed foods and sodas and is linked to weight gain and Type 2 diabetes.

Am J Clin Nutr April 2004 vol. 79 no. 4 537-543. George A Bray, Samara Joy Nielsen, and Barry M Popkin.

The American diet has spread into many countries and wherever it has been adopted there appears to be a decline in health and an increase in obesity!

7 Mexico

Another surprising result as the traditional Mexican diet is very healthy, but nowadays 1:3 are obese.

Less fresh and natural foods are eaten, having been usurped by lots of cereal and fizzy sodas. Everything changed in 1994 when Mexico signed a free trade agreement with the US. Since the influx of cheap calories from imported

American foods, they now have the highest rates of childhood obesity in the world and very poor dental health from all the sodas, candies and other processed foods.

6 Qatar

5 UAE

4 Saudi Arabia

3 Kuwait

All of the above Middle Eastern nations suffer from "New World Syndrome"!
Since striking oil and developing a taste for junk food, the ensuing obesity explosion throughout this part of the Middle East is down to a combination of both fast food and sedentary lifestyle.

2 Russia

The country with the penultimate worst diet in the world!

Another unexpected result, given that the national dish is beetroot soup and the Russians have a love for root vegetables.

But it's their love of alcohol which takes them to the bottom of the dietary pile, with 25% of men dying before 55 from alcohol poisoning, liver disease, accidents and drunken fights!

1 The South Pacific Marshall Islands

These exquisitely beautiful islands have the dubious honour of having the very worst diet in the world!

Seventy years ago the Marshallese islanders were hunter gatherers and diabetes was almost unheard of. Then in 1944 the US occupied the islands and the US government carried out nuclear tests on the Bikini Atoll. Unable to use their traditional hunting and fishing grounds any longer, the whole population became dependent on American imported foods. Their diet consists mostly of white rice, canned vegetables, lots of tinned fatty meat and turkey tails, which are 73% fat.

This appalling diet may also be coupled with a genetic predisposition to weight gain i.e. the islanders put on a lot of weight quickly during times of abundance so that they can survive during times of famine. But this survival technique now puts them at greater risk of diabetes and obesity!

Surprising and tragic in equal measure, the population of these coral atolls are some of the most obese people in the world with the highest death rate from diabetes.

The most useful information from this global picture of the eating habits of the world is that the more natural and unprocessed the diet, the better the health of the nation concerned. Conversely, the more processed the diet, the greater the likelihood of chronic disease and related death.

EAT
RESOURCES
Books

The Art of Eating Well
Jasmine Hemsley; Melissa Hemsley
Published June 2014
ISBN-13: 978-0091958329

Food is Better Medicine than Drugs
Patrick Holford
Published June 2007
ISBN-13: 978-0749927974
DVD
Released November 2007. Director Jake Seal

DVD's

Supersize Me
Released: January 2005. Director: Morgan Spurlock

Fast Food Nation
Released: August 2007. Director: Richard Linklater

Food, Inc
Released June 2010. Director. Robert Kenner

FAST

"Instead of using medicine, rather, fast a day."
Plutarch

FAST

BENEFITS

Rests and repairs the whole gastrointestinal tract.

Rests the liver.

Reduces appetite.

Maximises nutrition.

Increases energy.

Heals at a cellular level.

FAST
ACTION

NB Water fasting is not recommended as it is too extreme and can flood the system with toxins creating a "healing crisis".

Use organic produce.

Prepare for a fast by making changes several days beforehand
e.g. reduce then remove caffeine and animal products.

Plan the fast for a time when it is easiest for you to do it.

It is usually easier to fast when the weather is warm and pleasant rather than in the depths of winter.

Break the fast carefully, by introducing raw vegetables and fruit then salads and vegetarian soups and stews

Juice Fasting holidays are becoming popular. It's easier to juice fast when you are in a group, all juice fasting together in lovely surroundings and a lovely climate.

FAST

NB Intermittent Fasting for Weight Loss can be found under the title "Diet" and is not discussed in this section

Fasting has been a part of life since we first crawled out of the swamp! But was not necessarily of our own choosing!

Going from feast to famine has long been part of the human experience.

The quickest way to fast is through Juice Fasting, often used in naturopathic healing, although mainstream medicine does not recommend this!

Read on to see why fasting may be beneficial to your health!

Juice Fasting

This is fasting predominantly on freshly prepared raw vegetable juices, with a little freshly prepared fruit juice alongside herbs and spices for added nutrition and flavour.

Plant protein in the form of powdered algae is recommended, and this may help mitigate muscle loss and ensure a broad spectrum of vitamins and minerals, alongside those found in the juices.

Spirulina and/or chlorella are generally the natural plant protein supplements that are suggested.

Although anecdotally very effective, as can be seen in the film "Fat, Sick and Nearly Dead" (see Fasting: Resources), this is not for the faint-hearted!

My own experience of juice fasting was that, although effortless to do with a serious health problem, it became exponentially more difficult when the main problem appeared to be simply being overweight!

Both Joe Cross in the aforementioned film, and Jason Vale in "Super Juice Me" (see Fasting: Resources) had significant health issues and these may have been drivers to initially manage the regime of juice fasting. That they were male and younger and changed from appalling diets, also made success more likely.

But that in no way should take away from their exceptional achievement!

To continue, the health benefits needed to be significant!

An easy, if costly, way of trying this out is to go on a juice-fasting holiday! Having the juicing done for you in lovely surroundings, with exercise built in and in the company of others all in the same boat, is bound to be a great start to a juice fasting experience!

The two individuals in the films have undertaken long-term fasts, but you can gain significant benefits from shorter fasts, which can be done intermittently throughout the year. Care still needs to be taken to avoid losing muscle whatever the length of the fast, by adding plant protein to the juice, plus exercising at an appropriate level!

To continue to Juice Fast, the benefits would have to significantly outweigh the difficulties.

Long-term maintenance requires a high raw diet and juices, and throughout the fast and thereafter, it is really important to exercise to maintain muscle.

There are no clinical trials proving the efficacy of this kind of fast, but plenty of anecdotal evidence. As a well known healing technique in naturopathy, it is best undertaken under the supervision of a qualified naturopathic herbalist.

NB Water fasting is not recommended as it is too extreme and can flood the system with toxins creating a "healing crisis". This would feel something like having a viral infection such as influenza!

Conventional medicine is convinced that the body is designed to detoxify itself, but anecdotal evidence from individuals shows clearly the power of juice fasting.

Fasting is a powerful naturopathic healing tool. A fast consisting of raw fresh organic juices for 24 hours to detoxify is beneficial for most people, and could be done on a weekly basis, for one or two days. It can also be synchronised to the phases of the moon to be more successful.

At the extreme end of juice fasting is Joe Cross who features in his film and book, "Fat, Sick and Nearly Dead" which documents his 60 day juice fast. Not only did Joe lose 90 pounds with no excess skin issues, he also cured his chronic, unpleasant and painful skin condition, urticaria. Following the film's success, Joe founded "Reboot Your Life", a health and wellness company that helps people lose weight by teaching them how to incorporate more fruits and vegetables into their diets.

NB Joe's 60 day fast was medically supervised, as was the period after the fast when Joe follows an essentially raw vegan diet.

Wherever possible, the fruit and vegetables for fasting should be organically grown. For even a 1 day fast, it's best to choose a quiet day. Be well prepared with enough vegetables and fruit (80:20 vegetables to fruit). Fruit juice content needs to be low because of the issues with fructose and blood sugar levels. A natural laxative such as prune juice can be taken the evening before, or the morning of the fast. Herbal teas, spring or filtered water and potassium broth (a clear vegetable broth) can be taken throughout the day, and the juices taken to appetite.

All fasts, even if just for a day, need to be broken with care e.g. a day of fruits and vegetables, raw wherever possible, then adding soups and vegetable stews.

The much maligned "lemonade diet" is not a weight loss "diet" at all. This is a therapeutic fast and a powerful naturopathic cleansing treatment. Only lemon juice, cayenne tincture, maple syrup and water are taken as hot drinks throughout the day and it is used when you have an infection such as the common cold, influenza or any viral infection. It is best undertaken with the supervision of a qualified practitioner.

"Everyone has a physician inside him or her; we just have to help it in its work. The natural healing force within each one of us is the greatest force in getting well. Our food should be our medicine. Our medicine should be our food. But to eat when you are sick is to feed your sickness."

Hippocrates

FAST RESOURCES

DVD's

Fat, Sick and Nearly Dead
Released 2010 US. Director: Joe Cross

Jason Vale's Super Juice Me! Documentary
Released 2014. Director: Jason Vale

Books

The Reboot with Joe Juice Diet
Pub. January 2104
ISBN-13: 978-1444788327

7lbs in 7 Days: The Juice Master Diet
Jason Vale
Pub. April 2014
ISBN-13: 978-0007436187

Juice Fasting Retreats

http://healthybliss.net/international-directory-of-detox-juice-fast-healing-centers-and-retreats/

FORGIVE

"True forgiveness is one of the most healing, releasing and freeing gifts we give to ourselves."
Brandon Bays

"Forgiveness is the attribute of the strong."
Mahatma Gandhi

FORGIVE

BENEFITS

Peace of mind.

Forgiveness sets you free!

Lack of forgiveness has the potential to make you ill.

FORGIVE

ACTION

Forgive to set yourself free!

(You never ever have to forgive or condone anyone's behaviour.
It's the very essence of the person, their soul, that you forgive).

Forgive in your own mind and heart.
You don't need to have any physical contact with anyone else whatsoever.

Forgive yourself with the same compassion as for others.

Choose one of the forgiveness techniques within this topic and practice it.

Never allow the behaviour to occur again.

FORGIVE

I have found the concept of forgiveness to be very misunderstood, but this

one practice can totally transform your life!

And you do it for yourself!

To set yourself free!

You are never ever expected to forgive or condone any "behaviour"!

                      Never ever ever!!

Some behaviour is truly horrific. Whatever the level, it is never the behaviour that you forgive or condone.

Instead, it is the soul of the person.

Or, perhaps it's your own soul that needs forgiveness!

Forgiveness is not for the person you are forgiving. It is for yourself.

By forgiving you set yourself free.

To reiterate, you never ever ever have to condone behaviour. It is the very essence, the soul, of the person that you forgive.

Sometimes the person you most need to forgive is yourself

Just because you have forgiven someone, doesn't mean that you would ever allow bad behaviour towards you again.

You also don't have to ever have to have contact with them again.

This forgiveness takes place within your own mind and heart.

There is no time limit on forgiveness.

You can still practice forgiving someone regardless of whether they are still on the planet or not.

And the behaviour?
The Universe takes care of that!
Known as "Karma" in the East and "What goes around comes around" in the West.
Whatever you give out into the world: "in thought and word and deed" at some point returns to you.
Unless you wake up and remember who and what you really are…..

It took a huge amount of time for me to understand forgiveness!
Born into a Christian family, a religion where forgiveness is at the forefront of its' precepts, my

natural instincts were much more aligned to the older Judaic concept of:

"An eye for an eye and a tooth for a tooth".

Then, a major event happened in my life, and I found myself divorced and very very very angry!
Anger evolved to rage and revenge!
My head became a horrible place to live…..
At least I was able to recognise that something had to change!
I was aware that these emotions were beginning to produce physical symptoms and would soon create disease.
With no idea how to deal with these feelings, I also had absolutely no idea what to do.

By coincidence, my herbal teacher, Dr Kitty Campion, introduced me to "The Journey".

Totally resistant to the idea of mind/body healing, I went to a talk by Brandon Bays about "The Journey", but only after a huge amount of persuasion and with deep reluctance and cynicism.

From that initial talk, and still with a high degree of scepticism, I then took an appointment with the chief trainer at The Journey.

In less than four hours I was guided back to peace of mind and my own true self via this profound healing and forgiveness technique.

I certainly didn't make it easy for the practitioner! My default position is to know and understand a therapy, and I instinctively want to please the therapist.

Not this time!

He had to use every ounce of skill to work with me!
And I came away from the session totally changed forever!

I was then drawn back to this amazing mind/body healing technique again and again, becoming one of the first practitioners to train with Brandon Bays in 1999, and had already introduced Journey process work in my Herbal and Iridology practice for some time.
By introducing this technique to other people, either whilst in practice or just through word of mouth, I believe I have been able to guide people to make massive changes via this profound healing technique which focuses on forgiveness.

I use the technique on myself and friends nowadays, always with the same powerful results as that very first time.

Within each session an entire issue is completed and dealt with, and the results carry through to the future.

"You can't fake it (forgiveness). It has to come from an open heart. It has to be real. Otherwise it is pointless. In order to truly forgive, you must be willing to open your heart and face and release the pain there."

"It requires humility. It requires us to give up our righteous indignation, get off our soapbox, let go of blame, and let go of the pride of being right. It means we have to be willing to drop our victim

story, soften our stance, and if necessary, let our heart be broken wide open."

Brandon Bays

Another way to practice forgiveness is to do the following technique:

In this practice you first allow yourself to become very relaxed and then imagine yourself in a theatre watching a huge empty stage.

To this stage you bring everyone you have ever known - friends, family, teachers, workmates, bosses - everyone you can think of who has been part of your life. Then have them bow to you as the actors in the play of your life.

If they have affected you, it means that they played their part well!

Then say to them all: "I forgive you. Do you forgive me?" in the knowledge that you are not forgiving their behaviour, rather their souls.

You then let them all float away from the stage to grow and to continue their own path.

This simple technique alone can create massive change.

> *"All the world's a stage,*
>
> *And all the men and women merely players;*
>
> *They have their exits and their entrances,*
>
> *And one man in his time plays many parts,*
>
> *His acts being seven ages."*
>
> Shakespeare

Non-Personal Awareness (NPA)

"When you stop taking it personally, forgiveness is automatic."

Joel Young

Non-Personal Awareness (NPA) is described as a unique and powerful way to an easier life, a simple approach which allows you to easily stop suffering from taking stuff personally and live in peace.

The actual NPA process is just six lines long

"NPA is a 'Child of the new paradigm' - a brand new approach which 'shines the light' from a new angle and meets today's 'problem' energies with the speed, simplicity & quantum effortlessness they are calling for.

NPA stands for Non-Personal Awareness, and the little, 6 line, spoken-word, NPA process gracefully and powerfully threads into your consciousness, the awareness of the energetic nature of what you are focused on, and the realisation that it is not personal.

It's not personal because at a quantum level, infinite potential exists everywhere. To put that another way, everything exists everywhere simultaneously and we selectively experience that which we 'tune in to'. The impact of applying NPA is phenomenal. People are reporting huge shifts in consciousness, allowing them to experience relief and flow where they have been blocked for years, and an opening to allow their dreams to finally manifest."

Joel Young (Originator of NPA)

FORGIVE

RESOURCES

For books, CD's and seminars about the

The Journey

www.thejourney.com

For CD's, downloads and events about NPA

http://www.truthscompany.com/npacentral/npac-home.htm

HEAL

HEAL

BENEFITS

Each discipline (conventional medicine, alternative/complementary medicine and healing) has its own strengths.

Healing can be used alongside both conventional and alternative treatments

Used together, conventional medicine and alternative therapies and healing become more than the sum of the parts

HEAL

ACTION

Your health is your responsibility and the general maintenance of your physical body is down to you!

Breathe clean air (stop smoking!).

Drink pure water.

Eat nutritious food, organic whenever possible.

Get enough fresh air, exercise and sleep.

Meditate.

Practice gratitude and forgiveness.

Have fun!

Use the most appropriate form of medicine (conventional or alternative) alongside your lifestyle practices and practice healing on yourself or find a healer.

HEAL

There is a popular misconception that allopathic, alternative medicine and healing are all mutually exclusive, but harnessing all the resources that are available to you and finding the best from each will give you a greater chance of healing from any disease, be it physical, mental or emotional.

Each of them has strengths, but used together they are exponentially more powerful.

A clean environment, nutritious food, pure water and air are the bedrock underlying health. It is detrimental to the effectiveness of any healing technique if these conditions are not met first of all. We also have the issue of environmental toxins in our food, water and air that humanity has never had to deal with in previous generations. From herbicides and pesticides, growth hormones and antibiotics in our food, to chemicals leaching from plastics and non-stick surfaces.

Some of this "food" is really just a "food like" substance!

To maintain health, besides dealing with these basics, there's also your own genetics to take into consideration.

You are what you eat and drink, you are your lifestyle, you are what you think and believe and you are your microbiome!

Turns out you are also what your parents, grandparents, great-grandparents (and possibly even further back ancestrally), ate, drank, lived, thought, believed and what their microbiome was like!

Epigenetics is relatively new science, seriously studied for only a couple of decades.

What is epigenetics?

In a nutshell, it's additional information that is layered on top of the sequence of strings of molecules that make up DNA. So, you are not only a product of your inherited genes and lifestyle choices, you are also a product of your ancestors lifestyle and experiences.

Every cell in your body starts off with more or less the same DNA sequence. But a kidney cell doesn't need to follow the same part of the "instruction manual" as a liver or brain cell. But this additional information – epigenetics – is different! This additional information isn't fixed in the same way that the DNA sequence is. Some of this information can change throughout life, and in response to outside influences.

Any outside stimulus that can be detected by the body has the potential to cause epigenetic modifications. And some can be inherited! Studies of people whose ancestors survived through periods of starvation in Sweden and the Netherlands indicate that the effects of famine on health may influence at least three generations.

As the child of a mother subjected to semi-starvation from the age of 7 to 13 years of age, and emotional neglect throughout her childhood, I suspect that her health may have influenced mine.

It's possible that epigenetics will help us to understand much more about human health and disease.

Marcus Pembrey, emeritus professor of paediatric genetics at University College London, who was involved in the Swedish research said:

"you don't live your life just for yourself but also for your descendants. Although it is important to realise that transgenerational effects are for better as well as worse."

New "epidemics" such as autoimmune disorders or diabetes might be traced back to epigenetic markers left generations ago. A study of rats at the University of Texas suggests that soaring obesity and autism rates in humans could be due to "the chemical revolution of the Forties" i.e. our grandparents' exposure to new plastics, fertilisers and detergents.

David Crews, professor of psychology and zoology says:

"It's as if the exposure three generations before has reprogrammed the brain."

There could also be implications to what we eat. Pregnant women nowadays are advised to take folic acid, vitamin B12 and other nutrients containing "methyl groups", as these are believed to decrease the risk of asthma and brain and spinal cord defects in the foetus.

Misplaced epigenetic tags may cause certain cancers. Molecular biologists at Temple University in Philadelphia are currently investigating a potential alternative to traditional chemotherapy i.e. treating cancer patients with drugs that "reprogramme" cancer cells by reconfiguring the epigenetic markers.

There is also growing research that suggests it's not just physical characteristics or illnesses we might be passing onto future generations. It's possible that our DNA might even be affected by behavioural epigenetics too.

Allopathic Medicine

Allopathic Medicine is a system of medical practice that aims to treat disease by the use of remedies i.e. drugs or surgery. It is what we all understand mainstream medicine to be and is available from hospitals and medically trained doctors. Its greatest strength is in the treatment of emergencies, be they trauma or sudden health events.

If I were involved in a serious road traffic accident, I would want the microsurgery and anaesthesia, antibiotics, analgesics, sterile equipment and physiotherapy.

I'd also have the comfrey tea and the healing and meditation after the immediate crisis had been dealt with!

What I personally wouldn't want from allopathic medicine is to be "blanket medicated" on a just in case basis.

The pharmaceutical industry has a perfect business model, which may not always have your best interests at heart. Their ideal drug is one prescribed to a large amount of people, who will take the medication long term. There you have your repeat customer. They can also upsell further drugs to a proportion of these people (via their medical practitioner) which they need because of the side effects of the first drug!

The Alternatives

There are many alternatives to allopathic medicine and these are often better for chronic conditions which allopathic medicine is unable to help and may even have given up on.

Ideally the therapy deals with the lifestyle issues of eating, drinking, sleeping and exercise as part of the treatment, and you will probably be naturally drawn to the therapies that are likely to suit you best.

My introduction into this world was through herbalism, which seemed to make the most sense. It was obvious to me that certain plants had healing properties, as this was the foundation of modern pharmacology.

My herbal practitioner and teacher, Dr Kitty Campion, works as a naturopath, treating the whole person. Without her help, I don't think my daughter would ever have been born.

Dietary and lifestyle changes were made alongside the herbal treatment, which made perfect sense to me.

Healing

Things got a little cloudier for me when healing came into the picture.

My personal introduction was initially through the work of Louise Hay, and thereafter through The Journey with Brandon Bays.

But as a herbalist and iridologist, there had always been a small percentage of clients who didn't respond as well as could be expected from the treatment, despite their best efforts.

After having more "paints in my paintbox" with the mind/body healing techniques, I was now able to help virtually everyone at some level.

At this time I also "remembered" that I could heal - in fact I remembered that we all can! We all have the capacity to heal, but having spoken to other healers, some people may have more natural aptitude as healers. You can teach almost anyone to play the piano, but not everyone will become a concert pianist! However

I believe everyone has the capacity to heal himself or herself, and can be taught to do so.

Healing is also misunderstood. It may be that those being healed are not meant to remain on the planet and the physical aspect of the healing may appear not to have worked. That's not to say that it hasn't affected their emotional, mental and spiritual being and brought peace to them.

Integrated Medicine

Integrated medicine brings together conventional medicine with safe and effective complementary medicine. It emphasises the importance of the doctor-patient relationship and the use of all appropriate therapeutic approaches, healthcare professionals and disciplines to achieve healing and optimal health, with patients as active participants in their health care.

Integrated/Integrative medicine is an international movement. The US Consortium of Academic Health Centers for Integrative Medicine includes 44 academic medical centres, including Stanford, Yale, Johns Hopkins, Harvard and the Mayo Clinic. It aims

"to help transform medicine and healthcare through rigorous scientific studies, new models of clinical care, and innovative educational programmes that integrate biomedicine, the complexity of human beings, the intrinsic nature of healing and the rich diversity of therapeutic systems".

In the UK, The Royal London Hospital for Integrated Medicine (RHILM) is a leading institution in this growing, worldwide movement. The RHILM is part of University College London Hospitals NHS Foundation Trust and is Europe's largest public sector centre for integrated medicine. The hospital offers a range of therapies, which are fully integrated into the NHS and with conventional medicine.

HEAL

RESOURCES

Websites

www.bitesizehealth.com
www.truthscompany.com
www.thejourney.com

Books

You Can Heal Your Life
Louise Hay
Pub. July 2004
ISBN-13: 978-0937611012

Complete Dreamhealer
Adam McLeod
Pub. August 2009
ISBN-13: 978-0749929657

Quantum Healing
Deepak Chopra
Published November 1989
ISBN-13: 978-0553173321

Molecules of Emotion
Candace Pert
Pub. March 1999
ISBN-13: 978-0671033972

LIGHT

LIGHT

BENEFITS

Improved mood and energy levels.

Better sleep.

Improved immunity.

Improved libido.

Less risk of panic attacks.

Lower risk of diabetes and weight gain.

Lower risk of some cancers.

LIGHT

ACTION

Seasonal Affective Disorder (SAD syndrome) is a form of depression caused by a lack of light to the brain in winter in countries far from the Equator. Moving to a different climate would be effective if not practical.

However a winter holiday in the sunshine may be possible and beneficial.

Expose yourself to lots of bright light during the day, which improves sleep at night, as well as mood and alertness during daylight hours.

Exercise of any kind has been shown to be effective against depression. Activity is believed to change the level of the mood-regulating hormone serotonin in the brain. If you have a tendency towards SAD, outdoor exercise will have a double benefit, because you'll gain some daylight."

Use dim red lights for night-lights. Red light has the least power to shift circadian rhythm and suppress melatonin.

Avoid looking at bright screens beginning two to three hours before bed.

If you work night shifts or use a lot of electronic devices at night, consider wearing blue-blocking glasses.

For Seasonal Affective Disorder (SAD), a light therapy lamp used for 30-60 minutes each morning can improve mood and energy levels NB Light therapy lamps are not advised for bipolar or manic-depressive disorders (light therapy may cause a manic episode), for skin that is sensitive to light and medical conditions where the eyes are vulnerable to light damage.

St John's Wort is a herb that can improve SAD syndrome. It would be advisable to see a qualified herbalist rather than attempting to self-medicate as this herb can't be used in conjunction with light therapy because of a risk of photosensitivity.

LIGHT

Dr. Charles Czeisler of Harvard Medical School showed, in 1981, that daylight keeps a person's internal clock aligned with the environment.

We all have slightly different circadian rhythms which are physical, mental and behavioural changes that follow a roughly 24-hour cycle, responding primarily to light and darkness in our environment.

The average length is 24 and a quarter hours. The circadian rhythm of "owls" who stay up late, is slightly longer than "larks" where it is a little less than 24 hours.

Many studies have shown that working at night and exposure to light at night increases the risk of several types of breast and prostate cancer, diabetes, heart disease, and obesity.

Exposure to light at night suppresses the secretion of melatonin, a hormone that influences circadian rhythms.

A Harvard study indicated the possible connection to diabetes and possibly obesity. Ten people were put on a schedule that gradually shifted the timing of their circadian rhythms. Their blood sugar levels increased, throwing them into a prediabetic state. Levels of leptin, a hormone that leaves people feeling full after a meal, went down.

Even dim light can interfere with a person's circadian rhythm and melatonin secretion. Light at night is part of the reason that many people don't get enough sleep, and researchers have linked short sleep to increased risk for depression, diabetes and cardiovascular problem.

Any kind of light at night can suppress the secretion of melatonin, but blue light does so more powerfully.

Do you feel SAD during the winter months? SAD aka Seasonal Affective Disorder is a seasonal form of depression usually found in countries that have short daylight hours in winter.

Quick Symptom Check for SAD

You might have any or all of the following symptoms:

- low energy for everyday stuff e.g. work / study.
- difficulty concentrating.

- problems with sleep.
- depression i.e. feeling sad or "low"; tearful; guilty of letting yourself / others down; hopeless; despairing; apathetic; anxious; tense.
- panic attacks.
- mood changes in spring and autumn.
- overeating: particularly craving carbohydrates and putting on weight.
- prone to illness e.g. colds, infections, other illnesses.
- low libido i.e. loss of interest in sex.
- social and relationship problems i.e. irritability; not wanting to see people; difficult behaviour; abusive behaviour.
- alcohol or drug abuse.

NB If you have serious symptoms of depression at any time, you need to seek medical help.

So, what is Seasonal Affective Disorder (SAD)? SAD is thought to be linked to reduced exposure to sunlight during the winter, and sunlight can affect some of the brain's chemicals and hormones. It's thought that light stimulates that part of the brain (the hypothalamus) which controls mood, appetite and sleep, all of which affect how you feel.

SAD is mostly found in places such as Scandinavia, northern Europe, North America, North Asia, and in southern parts of Australia and South America. An estimated 2,000,000 people are affected by SAD in the UK and more than 12 million people across Northern Europe. Conversely, it's very rare to find anyone with

SAD symptoms living near the equator, where there's consistent sunlight all through the year. But people who have lived in the tropics and then move north are more vulnerable to developing SAD.

As with other types of depression, the two main symptoms of SAD are a low mood and a lack of interest in life with a tendency to be less active than normal and wanting to sleep more. With one of the other possible symptoms being a desire to eat more, particularly carbohydrates, it's little wonder that SAD at any level has the possibility to increase weight!

SAD is more common in women than men, with up to three times more women than men affected.

Most people affected have a mild version of SAD aka "the winter blues".

It makes winter feel miserable, and this is what this article mostly addresses. So, if you feel like you want to hibernate under your duvet during the winter and eat chocolate and buttered toast and lose all desire to go to the gym, you probably have SAD at this level.

LIGHT RESOURCES

Books

Winter Blues, Fourth Edition: Everything You Need to Know to Beat Seasonal Affective Disorder
Norman Rosenthal
Pub. Sept 2012
ISBN-10: 1609181859
ISBN-13: 978-1609181857

Products

SAD light therapy lamps
Blue light blocking glasses
Daylight light bulbs and lamps
are all readily available online

MEDITATE

MEDITATION

BENEFITS

Relaxation

Meditation prevents stress from getting into your system and simultaneously releases existing accumulated stress.

Inner Peace.

Increases happiness, creativity, imagination and enthusiasm.

Reduces anxiety.

Normalises blood pressure.

Decreases tension-related pain.

Improves immunity.

Connects you with your Higher Self.

MEDITATION

ACTION

Start small!

Just 5 minutes daily is better than a long period once a week.

Choose a type of meditation that appeals to you such as following a guided meditation, sitting in silence and following the breath, walking alone in nature, or chanting a mantra (see **www.bitesizehealth.com** for suggestions)

Choose a comfortable place where you won't be disturbed.

Sitting with your back upright is better than lying down, so that you are less likely to fall asleep. Unless you want to fall asleep!

Don't worry about "thinking"!

We are designed to think.
Let your thoughts pass through like clouds and don't attach to them.

Joining a group or go to a class to try out different types of meditation.

After a little practice, try meditating in unexpected places such as on public transport, in the middle of a busy shopping centre or in a medical waiting room.

If you can't sleep, meditate. It gives your brain the same benefits but in a shorter time. And you will probably fall asleep!

MEDITATE

About 30 years ago I went to a talk by Patch Adams (remember the film about him? Patch was played by Robin Williams). During the talk he told of his vision of a free hospital in Virginia in the US, and that when he's there he often goes fishing with friends who live locally and who don't generally know much about meditation etc. When asked about the meditation at his place, his reply informed me of the effortlessness of the process:

"Gee, it's kinda just like fishin'!"

From that simple sentence, I never got worried about whether I was doing it right, in the right position, doing the right kind of meditation etc. etc…

I am so grateful!

Over the years I've done many kinds of meditation from simply focusing on the breath, to guided meditations, to walking in nature, to practising mindfulness, to chanting in Sanskrit - sometimes for many hours.

Even silent retreats, sometimes for several days at a time.

Although, I still do all of the above, I now choose to live my life as much as possible as a walking, talking, breathing meditation. To reach this point it has been a transformative experience.

So what is Meditation?

It is thought by many that the purpose of meditation is simply to cope with stress. That's part of the picture, and very effective. But the real purpose of meditation is not to just de-stress, but to find peace within. This is the peace that spiritual traditions refer to as "the peace that passes all understanding".

Meditation enables you to get into the space between your thoughts.

This space between thoughts is the way to connect with the infinite mind, your core consciousness, the Universe itself.

This space is a field of infinite possibilities and pure potential. A space of infinite creativity and imagination, where everything is connected to everything. It is where there is something called the power of intention, which means intention is very powerful when brought to this space and creates it's own fulfilment.

This is what people call the Law of Attraction.

And these are the qualities of your own true self, your very spirit.

In meditation, you can access infinite possibilities, creativity, imagination, and power of intention. That's what meditation is really about.

To meditate, simply choose a place where you won't be disturbed and which is physically comfortable. Sitting is usually preferable to lying down, as with the latter you are likely to fall asleep!

Morning and evening are both good times to meditate as we are generally quieter then, but any time is good.

Thoughts will inevitably come into your mind.

That's normal! Just don't try to do anything with them, simply let them pass through like clouds in the sky and don't attach to them. By that, I mean that if you find yourself planning dinner, don't drive to the supermarket in your mind or find yourself mentally cooking the meal. If you become aware that you are thinking about what's passing through your mind, just return to focusing your awareness on your breath or the mantra and you will soon slip back into meditation.

When we pay attention to our breath, we are in the present moment. In an unforced, natural rhythm, just allow your breath to flow in and out, easily and effortlessly.

The effects of meditation are cumulative, and it's better to spend just a few minutes meditating every day rather than for longer periods only once a week.

Another way to meditate is to follow the same principles whilst walking in nature. This is a good way to meditate when you are feeling emotionally upset about something. You can meditate anywhere and anytime that your attention isn't required in the world.

Stress and Meditation:

Meditation prevents stress from getting into your system and simultaneously releases existing accumulated stress.

Physical Benefits of Meditation:

With meditation, your physiology undergoes changes and every cell in your body is filled with more energy, resulting in greater happiness, peace, enthusiasm.

Meditation also helps to lower blood pressure, reduce anxiety, decrease tension-related pain, improves mood and behaviour by increasing serotonin production, enhance the immune system and increases energy.

Mental Benefits of Meditation:

Meditation brings the brainwave pattern into an Alpha state, aiding in healing and with regular practice, anxiety decreases, emotional stability improves, creativity increases, intuition develops and you become happier, gaining clarity and peace of mind.

Meditation makes you aware that your inner attitude determines your happiness.

Mindfulness

Mindfulness is a form of meditation, growing in popularity, where the aim is to focus thoughts on the physical sensations of the body and detach yourself from the 'mind chatter'. Practising simple meditation techniques such as concentrating on your breathing helps build denser grey matter in those parts of the brain associated with learning and memory, controlling emotions and compassion.

Structural changes in the brain, large enough to be picked up by MRI scans were observed, and Dr Lazar commented:

"If you use a particular part of your brain, it's going to grow because you are using it. It really is mental exercise. Basically, the idea is "use it or lose it". It's like building a muscle." Dr Lazar's studied 16 volunteers who had their brains scanned before and after an eight-week 'mindfulness' course (weekly group sessions in which they did breathing exercises, gentle yoga and a 'body scan', focusing their thoughts on one part of the body at a time, plus practicing alone for 30 minutes daily).

MRI scans were taken before and after the sessions and compared with volunteers who had not taken part in the meditation.

After eight weeks, the meditators had thicker grey matter in several parts of the brain, including the left hippocampus, a small structure in the central brain involved in memory, learning and emotional regulation.

Other parts 'strengthened' included the posterior cingulate cortex, also important for memory and emotions; the temporo-parietal junction, involved in empathy; and the cerebellum, which helps coordinate movement.

The control group showed no structural brain changes.

Dr Lazar said mental exercise stimulated the neurons that make up grey matter to form denser connections among themselves.

At the Oxford Mindfulness Centre, Mark Williams (Professor of Clinical Psychology) says that mindfulness means knowing directly what is going on inside and outside ourselves, moment by moment. And that mindfulness can be an antidote to the "tunnel vision" that can develop in daily life, especially when we are busy, stressed or tired.

He said:

"It's easy to stop noticing the world around us. It's also easy to lose touch with the way our bodies are feeling and to end up living 'in our heads' – caught up in our thoughts without stopping to notice how those thoughts are driving our emotions and behaviour.

An important part of mindfulness is reconnecting with our bodies and the sensations they experience. This means waking up to the sights, sounds, smells and tastes of the present moment. That might be something as simple as the feel of a banister as we walk upstairs.

Another important part of mindfulness is an awareness of our thoughts and feelings as they happen moment to moment.

Awareness of this kind doesn't start by trying to change or fix anything. It's about allowing ourselves to see the present moment clearly. When we do that, it can positively change the way we see ourselves and our lives.

When we become more aware of the present moment, we begin to experience afresh many things in the world around us that we have been taking for granted.

Mindfulness also allows us to become more aware of the stream of thoughts and feelings that we experience and to see how we can become entangled in that stream in ways that are not helpful. This lets us stand back from our thoughts and start to see their patterns.

Gradually, we can train ourselves to notice when our thoughts are taking over and realise that thoughts are simply 'mental events' that do not have to control us.

Most of us have issues that we find hard to let go and mindfulness can help us deal with them more productively."

This kind of awareness also helps us to become aware of signs of stress or anxiety earlier, helping us deal with them better.
Reminding yourself to take notice of your thoughts, feelings, body sensations and the world around you is the first step to mindfulness.
"Even as we go about our daily lives, we can find new ways of waking up to the world around us," says Professor Williams.

"We can notice the sensations of things, the food we eat, the air moving past the body as we walk. All this may sound very small, but it has huge power to interrupt the 'autopilot' mode we often engage day to day, and to give us new perspectives on life."

He suggests that it can be helpful to pick a time e.g. whilst commuting on public transport or during a walk at lunchtime, then decide to be aware of the sensations created by the world around you. Trying new things, such as sitting in a different seat in meetings or going somewhere new for lunch, can also help you notice the world in a new way.

He goes on to say:

"Similarly, notice the busyness of your mind. Just observe your own thoughts. Stand back and watch them floating past, like leaves on a stream. There is no need to try to change the thoughts, or argue with them, or judge them: just observe. This takes practice. It's about putting the mind in a different mode, in which we see each thought as simply another mental event and not an objective reality that has control over us."

Mindfulness can be practised anywhere, but is particularly useful if you realise that you have been reliving past problems or living in future worries.

As well as practising mindfulness in daily life, mindfulness can also be practised formally, using meditation.

Several practices can help create a new awareness of body sensations, thoughts and feelings, and include meditation, yoga and tai chi.

MEDITATE

RESOURCES

Choose a type of meditation that appeals to you: following a guided meditation; sitting in silence and following the breath; walking in nature; chanting a mantra: see www.bitesizehealth.com for suggestions.

Guided Meditations

My personal favourite guided meditation is Brandon Bays "Healing Sand" and "Healing Light" which are especially suitable for newcomers to meditation and can be found on the Journey website:
www.thejourney.com

Chanting

You can download Deva Premal and Miten's beautiful chants from their website shop or buy their cd's. I particularly like their version of The Gayatri Mantra, which is also the theme to the TV series Battlestar Galactica:
www.devapremalmiten.com

For more chants see
www.bitesizehealth.com

MOVE

"Life is like riding a bicycle. To keep your balance you must keep moving."

Albert Einstein

"We do not quit playing because we grow old. We grow old because we quit playing"

Oliver Wendell Holmes

MOVE

BENEFITS

If you don't use it you lose it!

In this context, the loss refers to lean tissue aka muscle, without which you will get fatter and flabbier!

People who do regular activity have a lower risk of many chronic diseases: heart disease; type 2 diabetes; stroke; some cancers.

Physical activity can boost self-esteem, mood, sleep quality and energy, as well as reducing your risk of stress, depression, dementia and Alzheimer's disease.

MOVE

ACTION

Use it or lose it! 150 minutes of moderate intensity activity weekly is recommended for 19-64 year olds.

Choose an activity you really enjoy so that you want to do it.

Schedule physical activity into your diary as a priority.

Increase your non-exercise physical activity i.e. NEAT.

Use a rebounder.

Avoid sitting for long periods.

HIIT (High Intensity Training) can quickly get you fitter, and keep you fit, but you need to be Fit to do HIT.

MOVE

Nothing is more likely to send me head-first into a whole packet of chocolate digestives, than a lycra-clad fitness guru on television telling me that I would need to run for fifty minutes or more to burn off the calories in something like one small chocolate bar!

In fact, the whole concept sounds so depressing it's likely to send me straight back onto the sofa! They must know it doesn't work like that!! Instead exercise increases your metabolic rate for several hours, and so more calories are burned up following exercise.

I much prefer Paul McKenna's take on this, where he describes weight loss as creating a release of energy which needs to be channelled into something physically active and fun.

But what kind of exercise?
Anything that you want!

If it feels like fun you are much more likely to want to keep doing it!
Remember how much fun it was playing in snow? Nowadays you can do that year round in Snowdomes! And even in the desert in Dubai! Exercise doesn't have to be the nightmare of school-style sports, or gruelling gym sessions or "no pain, no gain" Fonda-style fitness.
Unless this is what you enjoy.

Children do most activity when it's not recorded! Not in formal games sessions at school or classes, but when they are playing!

Choose something that feels like playing and you'll be so much more likely to stick to it. So if dancing feels like fun – dance!

If swimming mind-numbing laps leaves you cold – swim instead at a water park, zipping down slides! Unless you like swimming laps…..

If you are older or very overweight, you may need to use your imagination a bit more!

You may find that your tastes have changed since you were eight years old – just go with the flow! The exercise that is the most fun for me personally, and apparently my tastes haven't changed that much….

over half a century on! My preference is still for water and slides!

But do something! Anything! You need to move!

Because….if you don't use it you lose it!

Exercise will help to keep your weight normal. But if you are already overweight, exercise alone will not be enough to create weight loss (especially if you are overweight and unfit already)

BUT

If you try to lose weight without exercise, you'll lose muscle and gain fat, ending up fatter and flabbier than you were to start with!

The Every Other Day Diet: Krista Varady and Bill Gottlieb

NB Before starting any exercise programme it's best to check first with your qualified medical advisor.

Any movement is useful, although some is more effective than others.

Choose something that you like to do and that matches your current level of fitness and funds.

Rebounding

One exception that I would recommend to everyone (as long as they have checked with their medical practitioner), is rebounding i.e. bouncing on a mini trampoline.

At a level appropriate for your fitness level and age. Just walking on it provides substantial benefits. It exercises you at a cellular level and moves lymph around, with the added benefit of increased immunity.

Unless you are already fighting fit, there are some forms of exercise that are more suitable for the over-fifties. You can stick with these or use them as preparation for more physically challenging activities as your level of fitness increases.

The much-maligned toning tables provide passive resistance exercise and certainly have their place in rehabilitation.

The most obvious form of exercise is walking, in any of its forms, and in many cases there is no cost involved. This can be enhanced by the use of Nordic walking poles to give an upper body workout simultaneously.

Next is gardening! And if you are lucky enough to have a garden to cultivate, by growing food crops you have the added bonus of home-grown food along with physical fitness.

Swimming is especially good if you are overweight as you can exercise more intensively with less risk to joints and bones as they are supported by the water. Although you still need to add in some weight bearing exercise to keep your bones strong.

Yoga is much misunderstood in Western culture, but at its most basic level, provides a series of stretching exercises and with regular practice is known to reduce stress, which is a major factor in weight gain for many.

Tai chi and Qi Gong increase energy (chi or qi) flow and improve health through gentle, graceful, repeated movements.

Pilates is an exercise system that focuses on stretching and strengthening the whole body to improve balance, muscle-strength, flexibility and posture. It was created by German-born Joseph Pilates in the early 1900s and incorporates elements of yoga, martial arts and Western exercises.

Dance is both exercise and an art form and usually involves rhythmic body movement to music. There are forms suitable for individuals, couples and groups with an equally broad range of physical intensity.

There are so many more forms of exercise, but the above are amongst those perhaps most suited to those of us who are overweight, unfit and not in the first flush of youth!

And how much exercise?

Well, the chart below gives you the recommended amounts for each age group, but more than that is fine!

Recommended physical activity levels according to UK government guidelines are:

- Children aged under 5 years should do 180 minutes daily.
- Young people (5-18 years) should do 60 minutes daily.
- Adults (19-64 years) should do 150 minutes every week.
- Older adults (65+ years) should do 150 minutes every week.

What a 60kg person burns in 30 minutes:

- running (6mph): 300 calories.
- tennis (singles): 240 calories.
- swimming (slow crawl): 240 calories.

- cycling (12-14mph): 240 calories.
- aerobic dancing: 195 calories.
- fast walking (4mph): 150 calories.

Source: Department of Health, 2004

But there's also another way to move:

Non-Exercise Activity Thermogenesis aka NEAT

What's NEAT?

Non-exercise activity thermogenesis is the energy that we use for everything that we do that's not sleeping, eating or sports-like exercise. And it would seem that our NEAT has decreased as our calorie intake has increased!

Nowadays many of us have to really think about how to incorporate any form of exercise into our lives, both formal exercise activities and NEAT! Adults and children alike have decreased their non-formal exercise exponentially. Many people have sedentary jobs, automation is increasing and it is customary to drive to and from work. Children are nannied and chaperoned throughout childhood, with their levels of NEAT eroded by understandable parental concerns about road traffic accidents and abduction. And there are many seductive technological alternatives to simple outdoor active play. We can't turn back the clock to a more organically active era, but we can take ideas from the past and come up with new creative solutions to improve our NEAT nowadays!

Here are my 7 ways to increase your NEAT!

1) Grow Your Own Food.
If you are lucky enough to have a garden or allotment, make growing food a priority. You can

do it alone or as a family, and you have a 2 for the price of 1 situation where you get organically grown food at minimal cost alongside the NEAT! Take it slowly if you are new to digging!

If you are doing this with children, giving them their own patch and letting them grow whatever they want to will help to enthuse them!

Another added benefit is that they may be more likely to want to try vegetables when they have been involved in growing them.

No access to a garden? See if you can find a neighbour, perhaps elderly, who can't manage their garden. Then offer an exchange of labour for 50% of the produce you grow using their garden. A win / win situation!

In my own distant childhood, my friend's Dad used to pay us all to weed the garden – 1p/bucket! With a very physically demanding job, he was grateful for the help and not only did it weed the huge vegetable garden it kept about half a dozen children busy for a whole Sunday afternoon whilst he was able to catch up with some sleep!

He had absolutely no need of any extra NEAT himself!

2) Walk to work and/or school.

Dr Krista Varady of "The Every Other Day Diet" fame, chooses to get off the train at a stop 2 miles from her university and to walk both ways each day! That's about 8,000 steps – only 2 thousand short of the recommended 10,000 per day. The extra 2000 would easily be taken up by general activity both at work and home.

This is an easy solution, mostly cost and risk free, and could be adapted into many people's lives with a bit of organisation.

3) Walk in your lunch break.

Depends a bit on the climate you live in and the area you work, but bringing a packed lunch and leaving the building to eat following a walk round the park or neighbourhood is another simple way to bring 3 helpful elements into your life: healthy food, light to the brain and physical activity!

Work from home? Take a formal active lunch break.

Go for a walk and eat something quick and healthy!

4) Take the stairs.

Rather than using the lift, walk to destinations if you are in an office building. And deliver messages in person rather than email across the room! Every little helps!

5) Drink 2 Litres of water daily.

Not only will this provide you with the benefits of hydration, you'll have the added benefit of having to get up out of your chair to go to the bathroom!

6) Make family time active.

Rather than sitting slumped in front of the TV *en famille* in the evening, go to the park or playground.

Or, if the weather is too unforgiving, play active games on things like an XBox or Wii.

This is now one of our family favourites, especially at Christmas, even though my kids are all grown ups!

And/or find activities that appeal to the whole family and do physically active stuff regularly – could be anything from hiking to cycling, to winter sports in a Snow-dome or swimming in anything from a municipal pool to a water park. At the weekend or in the holidays, choose activities that keep everyone moving! One relatively inexpensive way to do this for me is an annual membership to the local theme park and its accompanying indoor water park! Cheaper than gym memberships and a lot more fun for children!

Take a picnic so you don't ruin your efforts with the inevitable accompanying fast food temptations!

7) Choose active vacations.

There are all sorts of fancy expensive organised holidays that you can do that are naturally very active, from a winter sports holiday to sailing, or to a purpose built holiday centre like Centre Parks in the UK.

Even camping by a beach or in the countryside will keep everyone active, and is a fun and inexpensive solution with children.

And finally, to reiterate, whatever you do to increase your NEAT activity try and always make it fun, or at least something you don't mind doing until it's fully established as a habit!

High Intensity Training (HIT):

And then there's HIT…..

High Intensity Training (HIT) of just 3 minutes a week can give you as many of the health and fitness benefits of hours of conventional exercise. And these improvements can improve important health indicators within 4 weeks e.g. in some research centres insulin sensitivity in participants was improved by 24% on average. It's not suggested that HIT is all that you do, but just building more movement into your life along with HIT will improve your health and help with losing weight. This is the only "formal" exercise you need to do, along with more movement overall (walking or cycling to work if that's possible, taking the stairs instead of the lift, and adding any movement that is fun for you – dance, swimming – whatever!)

So, how does HIT work?

It's believed that HIT uses far more muscle tissue than classic aerobic exercise. When you do HIT, you are using not just the leg muscles, but also the upper body including arms and shoulders, so that 80% of the body's muscle cells are activated, compared to 20-40% for walking or moderate intensity jogging or cycling. And although not fully understood, it seems that HIT stimulates many of the same signalling pathways as those stimulated by endurance training.

BUT

How well HIT works may depend on your genetic makeup!

Everyone believes that exercise affects almost everyone in similar ways, but according to Dr Michael Mosley:

"The fact is that people respond to exercise in very different ways. In one international study, 1,000 people were asked to exercise four hours a week for 20 weeks. Their aerobic fitness was measured before and after starting this regime and the results were striking. Although 15 per cent of people made huge strides (so-called "super-responders"), 20 per cent showed no real improvement at all (non-responders").

There is no suggestion that the non-responders weren't exercising properly, it was simply that the exercise they were doing was not making them any aerobically fitter. Jamie Timmons, (Professor of ageing biology at Birmingham

University) and his collaborators investigated the reasons for these variations and discovered that much of the difference could be traced to a small number of genes. On the basis of this, they've developed a genetic test to predict who is likely to be a responder, and who is not.

Michael Mosley tested HIT himself and did the exercises on a stationary bike. He warmed up and then cycled to the maximum of his ability for 20 seconds, rested for a couple of minutes, and then went all-out for another 20 seconds, and then repeated this a third time. This totalled just a few minutes.

After four weeks and a total of 12 minutes of intense exercise plus 36 minutes of regular cycling on the machine, his insulin sensitivity had improved 24%. However, his aerobic fitness remained the same. He says:

"It turns out that the genetic test they had done on me had suggested I was a non-responder and however much exercise I had done, and of whatever form, my aerobic fitness would not have improved. I will continue doing HIT because I can see the benefits. It won't suit everyone, because although it is short, it is extremely intense."

Another study by scientists at McMaster University, Hamilton, Ontario in Canada found that HIT can deliver, in much less time, the same health benefits as moderate long term "endurance" training.

It's been known for years that doing regular moderate long term exercise e.g. cycling and running, for several hours a week, improves oxygen delivery to muscles and elimination of waste products and also improves the efficiency of fuel burning in the mitochondria. It also widens the blood vessels to the cells in muscle and increases the number of mitochondria they contain.

What that all means in practical terms is that you can do everyday things more effectively, with less strain, and lower risk of heart attack, stroke and diabetes.

The downside is the amount of time all this exercise takes. Professor Martin Gibala and his colleagues showed that you can get the same results in less time with short bursts of "HIT".

Professor Gibala also explains that

"We have shown that interval training does not have to be 'all out' in order to be effective."….

"Doing 10 x one-minute sprints on a standard stationary bike with about one minute of rest in between, three times a week, works as well in improving muscle as many hours of conventional long-term biking less strenuously."

In their previous research with college students they used an extreme set-up where the participants had to pedal to their absolute maximum capacity on a specially adapted lab exercise bike.

But in this new study they used a standard stationary bike and a workout that was still beyond the comfort zone of most people (about 95 per cent of maximal heart rate), but was only half of what might be regarded as an "all out" sprint.

This less extreme form of HIT should work well for people whose doctors may be concerned about them taking up the "all out" form: i.e. people who are older and/or unfit and/or overweight. An "all out" approach may not be safe or practical for many people and it was found that it was possible to get similar results with the more practical low-volume HIT (to 95% of maximum capacity).

If both the above levels of HIT are too intense for you, as they are for me, they are now working on developing HIT to help people who are overweight or who have metabolic disorders like diabetes.

To work out your maximum heart rate you take your age from 220.
So for me that's 220 minus 62 = 158
95% of 158 is 150
So my maximum heart rate is 158 bpm and 95% of my maximum heart rate is 150.

MOVE

RESOURCES

Rebounders are available online or in sports shops

YouTube has videos where you can learn anything from dance steps to Nordic walking to yoga. Or find classes or groups locally.

Use apps e.g. Runkeeper, to monitor your progress
Available from your app store.

Find an exercise buddy

Book:
(for HIT)

Fast Exercise
Michael Moseley
Pub. December 2013
ISBN-13: 978-1780721989

SLEEP

SLEEP

BENEFITS

Watching your weight can be as simple as getting enough sleep
(Lack of sleep can make you put on weight by drastically slowing your metabolism down).

Improved mood.

Improved concentration.

Improved athletic performance.

Better immune system.

Better memory.

Better sex life.

SLEEP

ACTION

Switch it off!

Go to bed!

Have a routine.

Sleep in the dark.

Have as little electronics as possible in the bedroom.

Work out how much sleep you need and have the right amount of sleep for you (usually 6 - 9 hours, occasionally between 4 - 10 hours).

Avoid caffeine in the evening but have a glass of water or a herbal tea just before sleeping.

Sleep in a well-ventilated room at the right temperature for you.

Sleep in a comfortable bed with suitable bedding.

Wake up naturally by going to bed early enough to get the amount of sleep you need. And with an alarm set as back up!

SLEEP

Switch it off!

It's soooo tempting to watch just another episode of that box set…...check email and Facebook one last time…...twitter on just a little longer….. No-one can make you stop but yourself - you're a grown-up now - honest! No electronics in the bedroom - or as little as possible.

Especially avoid watching the news just before going to sleep - whatever has happened it will keep till morning! Watching sad, frightening or tragic images repeatedly just before sleep is bound to have an impact on you at the deepest level, never mind affecting the quality of sleep itself.

Go to bed!

There are so very very many amazing distractions nowadays, it's so easy to want to carry on "playing" late into the night, but as said before….. Switch it off and go to bed!

It's a good idea to know how much sleep you personally need to feel and function at your best. And if you don't know, take a few nights to work out how many hours you need to wake up without an alarm and feeling good.

Then deliberately change your routine to make this happen for the majority of the time. There are times when this is virtually impossible: newborns; teething toddlers; flights to catch! So just do your best and nap in the day if you can, to make up for any sleep deprivation.

Make sure that you get the best quality of sleep that you can.

Besides the obvious stuff like a comfortable bed in a well-ventilated room, with both bed and room at the right temperature, the quality of sleep is better in a dark room and with no electronic paraphernalia flashing or beeping.

Sleep in the Dark

A group of cells in the hypothalamus in your brain controls your biological clock. Called the Suprachiasmatic Nucleus (SCN), these cells respond to light and dark signals.

Light travels through the optic nerve in your eye to your SCN, where it signals your body's clock that it's time to wake up. Light also signals your SCN to initiate other processes associated with being awake, such as raising your body temperature and producing hormones like cortisol.

When your eyes signal to your SCN that it's dark outside, you produce melatonin. The level of melatonin produced is related to the amount of exposure you have had to bright sunshine the previous day; the less bright light exposure the lower your melatonin levels.

Melatonin is a hormone that helps you sleep and radically decreases your risk of cancer. The more your sleep is disrupted with light, the lower your melatonin levels and the greater your risk of developing cancer becomes.

Melatonin is secreted primarily in your brain and at night it triggers biochemical activities, including a nocturnal reduction in your body's oestrogen levels. It's thought that chronically decreasing your melatonin production at night, which occurs when you're exposed to night time light, may increase the risk of cancer.

Sleep Med. 2007 Dec;8 Suppl 3:34-42.
Melatonin receptors: role on sleep and circadian rhythm regulation.
Dubocovich ML.

If you have problems sleeping, avoid caffeine later in the day.
Try chamomile tea before going to bed, and a couple of drops of essential oil of lavender on your pillow also helps with sleep issues.

The right amount of sleep for you personally, is critical for optimal health, and for most people it's one of the easier changes to make to improve overall health. Not getting enough sleep can be caused by a huge variety of reasons including the pace of life, problems with insomnia, a newborn or teething toddler or simply because of the vast amount of distractions available today!

How much sleep is enough?

Everyone needs to sleep and everyone has a unique sleep requirement. How much sleep depends upon genetic and physiological factors, and also varies by age, sex, and previous sleep amounts.

So, enough sleep is the amount that allows you to wake up spontaneously, feeling refreshed and alert and ready for the day ahead. For most adults that's generally between 6 and 9 hours each night, but there are individuals who need more or less.

Why do we sleep?

We still don't really understand the exact function of sleep, and it's thought that sleep may serve many purposes.

Sleep deprivation makes us feel sleepy and results in poor performance. Whereas enough sleep improves our alertness, mood, and performance. Sleep may also provide significant long-term health benefits, but there may also be many modifying factors such as the age, duration of sleep, influence of co-existing health problems and lifestyle and environmental factors.

The exact amount of sleep sufficient for optimal performance of a task may vary depending upon the task that is being performed, the time of day the task is performed, and the level of performance required.

Whilst we sleep, dreams may be clues for when we're awake.

Not getting enough sleep is believed to contribute to weight gain.

If you eat before you go to sleep it's been shown that this impacts on the quality of sleep by negatively affecting hormones that affect healing i.e. Human Growth Hormone, Testosterone and Erythropoietin.

Sleep and weight gain.

Think that fat is an inert gloop that just sits there and won't budge?

Wrong!!

It's actually the largest endocrine glands in the body.

Fat secretes a hormone called that tells you when you are full.

That hormone is called Leptin!

Leptin (along with another hormone, ghrelin), is responsible for regulating the balance of energy in the body by indicating when it is hungry and when it is full.

Leptin affects body weight and is secreted primarily by fat cells, and signals the hypothalamus about the amount of fat storage in the body. Decreased leptin tells the body there is a shortage of calories and makes you hungry, while increased levels promote energy expenditure.

Ghrelin is secreted by the stomach and stimulates appetite, increasing appetite before meals.

A recent study looked at nocturnal levels of leptin and ghrelin.

These two hormones, which are primarily responsible for regulating the body's energy balance, tell the body when it is hungry and when full.

The study found that chronic insomnia disrupts one of these two hormones, ghrelin, and shows how diverse behaviours like sleep and eating are connected, and highlights the importance of a good night's sleep for the body.

Psychoneuroendocrinology. May 2009; 34(4): 540–545.

Published online Dec 6, 2008. doi: 10.1016/j.psyneuen.2008.10.016

PMCID: PMC2725023

NIHMSID: NIHMS118452

Nocturnal levels of ghrelin and leptin and sleep in chronic insomnia

Sarosh J. Motivala, A. Janet Tomiyama, Michael Ziegler, Srikrishna Khandrika, and Michael R. Irwin.

SLEEP

RESOURCES

Chamomile tea.

Available from health food shops, supermarkets and online.

Essential oil of lavender.

Put a couple of drops on your pillow at night.

Available online or from health food shops.

Book and CD

I Can Make You Sleep
Paul McKenna
Pub. January 2009
ISBN-13: 978-0593055380

Emotional Freedom Technique (EFT)
www.emofree.com
free online resource or to find a practitioner

THANK

"The past is history, the future a mystery, this moment is a gift. That's why they call it the present"

THANK

BENEFITS

The more you feel and express gratitude, the more grateful you will feel.

The more you feel gratitude and say thank you, the more things come to you!

THANK

ACTION

Start a regular practice of gratitude.

Before you sleep:
Go through in your mind everything that you have to be grateful for.
Think about your day and remember the very best part of it, however small.

Write a list of everything you have to be grateful for and why.

Practice gratitude especially when you are experiencing difficulties.

THANK

"Count your Blessings" when all is well in your world is easy, though most forget!

If you are going through challenging circumstances it can be difficult to do and "Count your blessings" can sound trite. This is when you need to do it all the more to help facilitate changes!

That's not to say you should squish down any feelings of anger, despair, grief, sadness or whatever it is that you have reason to feel.

If you just allow yourself to experience the pure emotion. it will pass!

It only sticks to you like glue if you attach story to the feelings.

And then you can stay in the feeling of that emotion indefinitely!

So in order for things to change, once you have allowed yourself to fully experience the feelings associated with whatever is happening in your life, feelings of thankfulness for what you do have will help bring about change more quickly than anything else you can do.

I learned this the hard way and the opposite way around!

The more ungrateful I was, the more it felt like my life was being taken apart piece by piece and that all the good in it was leaving. And I am eternally grateful to the people who guided me back to a more positive and grateful attitude.

Counting Your Blessings

"If you woke up this morning with more health than illness… you are more blessed than the million who will not survive this week.

If you have never experienced the danger of battle, the loneliness of imprisonment, the agony of torture, or the pangs of starvation… you are ahead of 500 million people in the world.

If you can attend a church meeting without fear of harassment, arrest, torture of death… you are more blessed than 3 billion people in the world.

If you have food in the refrigerator, clothes on your back, a roof overhead and a place to sleep… you are richer than 75% of this world.

If you have money in the bank, in your wallet, and spare change in a dish someplace… you are amongst the top 8% of the world's wealthy. If you hold up your head with a smile on your face and are truly thankful… you are blessed because the majority can, but most do not.
If you can hold someone's hand, hug them or even touch them on the shoulder… you are blessed because you can offer a healing touch…."

I've been unable to find the author of this powerful piece, or validate the figures therein. But even if not absolutely accurate, it feels close enough to deliver the message

THANK

RESOURCES

The Magic
Rhonda Byrne
Pub. March 2012
ISBN-13: 978-1849838399

Secret Gratitude Book
Rhonda Byrne
Pub. December 2007

ISBN-13: 978-1847371881

Gratitude: A Way of Life
Louise Hay
Pub. August 2004
ISBN-13: 978-1561703098

THINK

"Thoughts Become Things...Choose The Good Ones!"

Mike Dooley

THINK

BENEFITS

Become a co-creator of your life along with the Universe, by the use of your thoughts, words and deeds.

Stay open to all possibilities...

Things that happens to us in life are not necessarily what they seem to be on the surface!

THINK

ACTION

Thoughts become things!
Be careful what you think about!

Thoughts become things!
Be careful what you talk about!

Thoughts become things
Be careful what actions you take!

Visualise what you want and then imagine yourself as if it has already come to pass.
Say thank you as though you already have it.

Everything you think about, talk about and do will take you in the direction of your dreams……

Or not, depending on what it is that you are thinking about, talking about and doing…..

Take action in the direction of your dreams, whilst not planning the minutiae of the journey or the exact outcome.

Taking action is key to making the "thinking" part work!

THINK

The Old Man and The Horse (Chinese proverb)

Once upon a time, there was an old man who lived in China.

A good man, he had a son whom he loved dearly. Both father and son loved horses and loved to ride whenever possible.

One day a stable door was accidentally left open and one of the old man's favourite stallions escaped. When people heard the news they all said how sorry they were to hear of this misfortune. To their surprise the old man didn't react how everyone expected at all! He replied saying that losing the horse wasn't necessarily bad luck at all! There was no way to predict that the horse would escape, it just happened. And now there was nothing that could be done about it. When they said they were sorry about his misfortune he simply said:

"We'll see..."

And a month later, the stallion came back! But not alone! He brought with him a beautiful mare.
When everyone heard the news they rushed to congratulate him. But again, he simply said:

"We'll see…"

A few days later the son was out riding, when the mare slipped and fell. The young man's leg was crushed so badly in the fall it he was unlikely he'd make a full recovery and would always walk without a limp. Again people sympathised with the old man for his bad luck. Someone suggested that the old man sell the mare before any more bad luck could happen, and another even said that he should kill the mare in revenge. But instead he simply said yet again...

"We'll see…"

Months went by, and then war broke out. The army came to the area and all of the young men were conscripted, except for the old man's son. Nearly all died in the ensuing battles. But the injured young man was left behind at home, the sole survivor!

Sometimes when something happens that appears to be good luck, the end results are not as good as expected. And sometimes, what appears at first sight to be misfortune has a surprisingly happy outcome….

The things of this world are rarely what they seem to be on the surface!

Which brings us to the Laws of Attraction and Action…..

The Laws of Action and Attraction?

The "Law of Action" is the way of achieving what you want in life by your own efforts.

The "Law of Attraction" uses your power to visualise what it is you want in life as if you already have it.

"There are only 3 things that can make your dreams come true: Your thoughts, your words and your actions!" Mike Dooley

The Law of Action alone is a very hard path. You may end up with the results you want, but usually only with a huge amount of effort. This is the "hard work" way to success! A path not only trodden by many, it's also believed by many to be more than necessary, but "good for the soul"!

Exposed to this way of thinking throughout my early years, it instilled a feeling that nothing was of value if you hadn't had to work hard for it! Which meant that however hard I worked, in order to be more successful I would have to work even harder…..

But I didn't arrive on the planet with the physical or mental resources to sustain this way of living indefinitely, and, although I did my best, it often left me exhausted or ill, even as I achieved success.

And it slowly dawned on me that the people who were the most successful were not necessarily the people who were working the hardest. In fact it became increasingly obvious that some of the people working the hardest on the planet were some of the most materially poor…..

At the same time, throughout my life, I was already using the "Law of Attraction" unwittingly. Stuff and circumstances that I dreamed of and wished for quite often turned up in my life.

But randomly and unpredictably!

So I have been using both the Law of Attraction and the Law of Action all my life, but for many years without a clue about what I was doing!

Once I knew about the Law of Attraction, I was bewildered by the fact that sometimes the results were breathtakingly accurate, and sometimes completely bewildering.

And sometimes absolutely nothing happened at all!

It eventually dawned on me that these two laws work synergistically.

If you do absolutely nothing but visualise, absolutely nothing is likely to happen!

Except occasionally and randomly.

And if you simply use your will to make stuff happen, it may very well do so, but may also take enormous effort.

Harnessing action to imagination is what makes the magic happen and allows you to be a co-creator with the Universe!
Visualise what you want as if you already had it. Express gratitude as if you already have already received it, and then take action.
This is the magic formula for manifestation.

But there's a caveat to this!
Don't try and work out exactly how your vision will come to pass. Just take small steps in the direction of your dreams and allow the Universe to do the rest. Being too prescriptive can mess

things up, potentially blocking amazing things from happening.

THINK

RESOURCES

Books:

The Secret
Rhonda Byrne
Pub. August 2013
ISBN-13: 978-1471130618
Plus
The Secret DVD
Rhonda Byrne

Begin with Yes
Paul Boynton
Pub. October 2009
ISBN-13: 978-1448691623

Leveraging the Universe: 7 Steps to Engaging Life's Magic
Mike Dooley
Pub. January 2013
ISBN-13: 978-1582703152

THE END

No, not the end of the book - the end of your life!

We only have this moment!

"Dream as if you'll live forever, live as if you'll die today."

James Dean

None of us know when whether we will live for the biblical three score years and ten (aka 70 years).

Or the increasingly commonplace four score years and ten - or even more (aka 90+ years)

Or just today!

Bronnie Ware, author of "The Top Five Regrets of the Dying" writes:

"For many years I worked in palliative care. My patients were those who had gone home to die. Some incredibly special times were shared. I was with them for the last 3 to 12 weeks of their lives.

People grow a lot when they are faced with their own mortality. I learnt never to underestimate someone's capacity for growth. Some changes were phenomenal. Each experienced a variety of emotions, as expected, denial, fear, anger, remorse, more denial and eventually acceptance. Every single patient found their peace before they departed though, every one of them.

When questioned about any regrets they had or anything they would do differently, common themes surfaced again and again. Here are the most common five:

1. I wish I'd had the courage to live a life true to myself, not the life others expected of me.
This was the most common regret of all. When people realise that their life is almost over and look back clearly on it, it is easy to see how many dreams have gone unfulfilled. Most people had not honored even a half of their dreams and had to die knowing that it was due to choices they had made, or not made.
It is very important to try and honour at least some of your dreams along the way. From the moment that you lose your health, it is too late.

Health brings a freedom very few realise, until they no longer have it.

2. I wish I didn't work so hard.

This came from every male patient that I nursed. They missed their children's youth and their partner's companionship. Women also spoke of this regret. But as most were from an older generation, many of the female patients had not been breadwinners. All of the men I nursed deeply regretted spending so much of their lives on the treadmill of a work existence.

By simplifying your lifestyle and making conscious choices along the way, it is possible to not need the income that you think you do. And by creating more space in your life, you become happier and more open to new opportunities, ones more suited to your new lifestyle.

3. I wish I'd had the courage to express my feelings.

Many people suppressed their feelings in order to keep peace with others. As a result, they settled for a mediocre existence and never became who they were truly capable of becoming. Many developed illnesses relating to the bitterness and resentment they carried as a result.

We cannot control the reactions of others. However, although people may initially react when you change the way you are by speaking honestly, in the end it raises the relationship to a whole new and healthier level. Either that or it releases the unhealthy relationship from your life. Either way, you win.

4. I wish I had stayed in touch with my friends.

Often they would not truly realise the full benefits of old friends until their dying weeks and it was not always possible to track them down. Many had become so caught up in their own lives that they had let golden friendships slip by over the years. There were many deep regrets about not giving friendships the time and effort that they deserved. Everyone misses their friends when they are dying.

It is common for anyone in a busy lifestyle to let friendships slip. But when you are faced with your approaching death, the physical details of life fall away. People do want to get their financial affairs in order if possible. But it is not money or status that holds the true importance for them. They want to get things in order more for the benefit of those they love. Usually though, they are too ill and weary to ever manage this task. It is all comes down to love and relationships in the end. That is all that remains in the final weeks, love and relationships.

5. I wish that I had let myself be happier.

This is a surprisingly common one. Many did not realise until the end that happiness is a choice. They had stayed stuck in old patterns and habits. The so-called 'comfort' of familiarity overflowed into their emotions, as well as their physical lives. Fear of change had them pretending to others, and to their selves, that they were content. When deep within, they longed to laugh properly and have silliness in their life again.

When you are on your deathbed, what others think of you is a long way from your mind. How wonderful to be able to let go and smile again, long before you are dying.

Life is a choice. It is YOUR life. Choose consciously, choose wisely, choose honestly. Choose happiness."

And then what?……

……the next great adventure begins!

THE END

RESOURCES

Books

The Top Five Regrets of the Dying
Bronnie Ware
Pub. March 2012
ISBN-13: 978-1848509993

The Top Ten Things Dead People Want to Tell You
Mike Dooley
Pub. October 2014
ISBN-13: 978-1781803943

"We are part of this Universe…

We are in this Universe…

But perhaps more importantly than both of these facts…….

The Universe is in us!"

Neil deGrasse Tyson

Made in the USA
Charleston, SC
08 December 2014